God Makes Love, Truth, and Holiness Work

Facts and Fictions for Pre-puberty Tweens in a Messed-up World

by Al Hiebert, PhD

illustrated by Claudia Castro Castro

19-100 Home St. N.
Steinbach, MB, Canada R5G 2G9

Library and Archives Canada Cataloguing in Publication

Hiebert, Al, 1940-, author
God makes love, truth, and holiness work : facts and fictions for pre-puberty tweens in a messed-up world / Al Hiebert ; Claudia Castro Castro, illustrator.

(Growing up in Christ)
ISBN 978-0-9868515-5-1 (paperback)

1. Christian life--Juvenile literature. 2. Children--Religious life--
Juvenile literature. I. Castro Castro, Claudia, illustrator II. Title.

BV4571.3.H55 2016 j248.8'2 C2016-903195-0

Cover design by Gordan Blazevic

Dedicated to those kids who wish to grow up in Christ
and to their parents

Truth does not become more true by virtue
of the fact that the entire world agrees with it,
nor less so even if the whole world disagrees with it.
– Moses Maimonides, *Guide for the Perplexed*
(about 1190AD).

CONTENTS

To the parents

God gave you and your kids the gift of sexuality to serve as a blessing and a source of much joy in your family to His greater glory.

No one knows your kids better than you do. No one knows better than you at what age and in what language sensitive topics (for example, sex and bullying) should be discussed with them. Your unique love, knowledge, and concerns for your kids give you a priceless privilege and an awesome responsibility for their wholesome Christian nurture. But sex is such a precious and private gift of God in married life that most parents find such discussions with their growing kids uncomfortable. One recent text reports, "Only about 15 percent of adolescents have had conversations about sexuality with their parents."[1] This series of six books seeks to correct this need sensitively and under parent direction. It is intended to equip Christian parents to empower their kids to grow up in Christ in a messed-up world. Book One (*A is for Adam*), geared for ages two to five, is a colourful alphabet nursery rhyme treatment of Bible characters and family principles. The *A is for Adam Coloring Book* has the same text. Book Two (*The Kids of Messed-up Woods*), for early readers ages five to eight, continues many of these concerns in a "first chaptered novel" format. Book Three (*God Makes Truth, Love, and Holiness Work*) is for pre-puberty "tweens," in middle school. Book Four (*Dealing with Doubts and Differences*) is for teens. It is a series of essays on common challenges kids face in high school and university. Book Five (*Deciding Right from Wrong*), also for teens, focuses on grey ethical issues they need to address in a secular world.

All the materials in this series promote a biblical perspective. Some parts discuss current medical science. Each book can be used in isolation from the others. Whether or not you have read the first or second book, perhaps you have already introduced them to a biblical perspective on bullying and sex in the context of God's perfect creation, which was messed up by human sin, then redeemed by Christ's atonement and completed in heaven for those who accept

God's gift of salvation by repentance and faith. This book is written in an email dialogue form with siblings Brook and Ryan, now four years older than they were in Book Two. Special thanks to friend and writer Barbara Ann Derksen for her contributions to the "Ms. Barb" responses to many of Brook's queries and to copy editor Audrey Dorsch for her contributions to the quality of the text.

This age-graduated series is designed to help you *start conversations* with your kids about the foundations of a wholesome Christian life in the midst of a growingly hostile secular culture. Becoming Christ-like whole teens through the challenges of puberty is the theme here. Your kids need to see themselves and other people as created in God's image, and thus deserving of our love and respect, even when they mess up. They need to learn to come to you first with their questions about life and the world around them. The dialogue boxes "At Our House" facilitate wholesome Christian nurture at your discretion. A Parents' Appendix suggests further ideas and Internet resources to help you in these discussions and to answer your kids' questions. Be sure you read this book first before you read it with your kids (or have them read it on their own).

Parenting is always risky. So is marriage. Even "experts" look for help. This series should build your confidence in this world-changing challenge. Happy, healthy Christian kids learn godly wisdom mostly from loving and caring Christian parents before secular influences shape their kids' values. As a parent, you should be the first to talk with your kids about bullying and sex, but only after you have talked with your spouse about it. Don't expect your kids to approach you about sensitive topics before you have talked with them about such matters. Sure, most parents would much prefer that their kids stay young and innocent. Our culture really does not permit that any more. Sadly, many in our culture dismiss biblical convictions on sex as bullying. Why should we be surprised if our culture shapes our kids' understandings and values about sensitive topics? "Our job as Christian parents is not to become our kids' best friend; it is to produce thriving disciples of Jesus Christ who are following God in all they think, say, and do."[2]

Your kids' participation in various church programs and involvement with Christian family, friends, and media should reinforce biblical values. Influences also come from non-Christian family and friends, secular media, and schools. Your kids will make their own choices on values during their growing up years. Some may not be as wholesome as you might wish. Some governments reject parents' right to serve as their children's primary educators on moral issues. We need to counter this trend (2 Corinthians 10:3–5). Sadly, some Christian parents just lean on secular influences and kids' questions. But why let secular influencers teach your kids false beliefs about morals that you then need to correct later?

Young children are naturally parent oriented. Too quickly they become primarily peer oriented, when they may pick up secular values that may mess them up. Many believe that secular sex education and anti-bullying education without a biblical creation-fall-redemption-consummation theological context does our kids a great disservice. These often prompt premature exploring and sexual experimenting that messes up too many kids, sometimes temporarily, sometimes for life. Secular influences may also prepare them for inappropriate sexual touching and for sexual abuse, in person or via electronic media. Your kids are in urgent need of biblical convictions and strategies for dealing with very serious threats in this area.

Since public education is pushing secular views of sex and bullying into more areas than we might like, it may be wiser to raise these sensitive issues with your kids just a bit too early rather than a bit too late. God knows the "perfect" time for each child; we don't. Studies show that most parents wait too long, or never deal with some of these issues at all.

This book deals with a wide array of issues, some of which may not be suitable for every 8- to 12-year-old tween. Depending on many unique factors, some kids under 8 may be ready to deal with some of these issues; others at 12 may not yet be ready. As a parent, you should not hesitate to regulate the timing, the process, and the language in which these issues are discussed. Some issues you might prefer not to discuss at all, were it not for the messed-up culture of our time. Most 8- to 12-year-olds are likely to be ready to deal with most or all of these issues at some time during that period. Likely the most challenging issues for many tweens, especially for the younger ones, are those in Chapters 8 to 11. On some issues you might disagree with the views taken here. In that case, kindly indicate your concerns on the "Contact" page at www.growingupinchrist.com.

Developmental psychologists and Christian kids' ministries specialists agree with the Bible, that nurturing kids' values is an every-day process, not limited to special times, such as when reading a book or going to church or school. In Proverbs 22:6 God instructs parents: Start children off on the way they should go, and even when they are old they will not turn from it (NIV). In Deuteronomy 6:7 God tells us how to teach kids His moral expectations of us all: Impress them on your children. Talk about them when you sit at home and when you walk along the road, when you lie down and when you get up (NIV). The "At Our House" exercises should help you with that. They are designed to strengthen the love-bond attachment of your kids to you and to deepen your insights into your kids' thoughts and experiences.

Here are several closing suggestions:

1. **Take it slow,** especially the first time reading this with your child, perhaps no more than a chapter at a time.

2. **Encourage questions.** You are your kids' best experts on bullying, sex, and all sensitive issues. If you are stumped, ask for research time. Check resources in the Parents' Appendix. If you are still stumped, contact us on the "Contact" page at www.growingupinchrist.com.

3. **Keep Calm.** God designed sex as an intensely intimate, private, and precious experience. Hence, some embarrassment is perfectly appropriate. Never let that suggest that it's dirty. It's too sacred.[3] God gave you and your kids the gift of sexuality to serve as a blessing and a source of much joy to His greater glory.

Enjoy this precious time of your life and of theirs!

1 GOD MAKES LOVE, TRUTH, AND HOLINESS WORK

Hi, Brook and Ryan

Congratulations, you are both about to enter one of the most exciting and challenging stages of your life. It's a time when you will make many changes, some of which you can control, others you can't. It's all about growing up into adulthood! Depending on how you choose in the areas you can control, you will either grow up in Christ or you may grow up messed up or broken, as too many kids do these days.

You may be reading this book and discussing ideas with your parents because both you and they much prefer (as God does) that you grow up in Christ. What does that mean? Simply it means that you will mature into the young woman or man God wants you to be.

Will you make some mistakes along the way? Likely, yes; most kids do; perhaps all kids do. But the fewer mistakes you make and the less serious they are, the more quickly you'll recover from them and still grow up in Christ.

Because we all live in a fallen, sinful world as fallen, sinful people, we all mess up sometimes[4] but thanks to God's grace, the instructions of the Bible and the direction and power of the Holy Spirit, we can turn from our sin (repent)[5] and claim the victory over sin in the power of Jesus' atonement for our sin.[6] Later you will read about mistakes that kids your age sometimes make, and how to deal with these so that if you make them or see others make them you know how to get back on track to growing up in Christ. You will also read about various falsehoods that some fine people may urge you to believe, and you will learn how to deal with them. The "At Our House" boxes contain some questions you might like to discuss with your parents. Some of these are debated in our culture. A few are even debated in some of our churches. Part of growing up is to establish your own convictions about what is really true about these issues. That's why it's wise to discuss these matters with your parents. There's also a Parents' Appendix to give suggestions on these questions (which you may read, if you like). Such family discussions can be crucial to strengthening the trust and family ties that are absolutely essential to smooth sailing as you mature to adulthood.

Much of what you'll read here relates to Christian character development. This is the part you can control for yourselves, Brook and Ryan – so you both need to read those chapters. The part you mostly cannot control for yourselves is how your bodies will change through puberty as you mature to adulthood. You'll see separate chapters for each of you on these topics, though you are welcome to read each other's mail, so you can better understand the unique challenges that girls and boys face as you grow up. Medical terms new to you are briefly defined in the text and in the Glossary/Words to Know section just before the Parents' Appendix. A few medical facts may differ from what other authorities (such as media and schools) want you to believe. In discussion with your parents, you need to decide which ideas you will embrace as true. Remember, when authorities disagree, God knows the truth, even if others say differently.

Remember, God invented the universe to be very good, though people messed it up with our sinful rebellion.[7] Also, human sin put a curse on nature, so our world is not as God created it to be, both in the personal moral/spiritual realm and in the physical/natural realm.[8] Remember, God created a beautiful universe and all the good things in it to work together, including our first parents, Adam and Eve in the Garden of Eden. God created Adam and Eve in His own image. This means they were persons, with mind, emotion, and will, somewhat like God. Since God is spirit, He does not have a body like we do. But since God is love, and love is an interpersonal relationship, He wants us to love and respect Him and to love and respect all our fellow humans, as God also loves all people, including those who hate and reject Him. We need to do the same, regardless that people sometimes act mean and treat us and others with hate.

If anyone tells you all world religions are basically the same, you can reply that the God of the Bible is the only deity among about 1,200 world religions who loves His enemies. He's also the only deity who commands His followers to love our enemies. The Bible uses several words for love. They don't all mean enthralled affection and romance, as too many people think these days.

Meditate on a few Scriptures about God being love and so should we be.

> 1 John 4:7–11: Dear friends, let us continue to love one another, for *love comes from God.* Anyone who loves is a child of God and knows God. But anyone who does not love does not know God, for *God is love.* God showed how much he loved us by sending his one and only Son into the world so that we might have eternal life through him. This is *real love* – not that we loved God, but that he loved us and sent his Son as a sacrifice to take away our sins. Dear friends, *since God loved us that much,* we surely *ought to love each other.* (Emphasis added.)
>
> John 13:35: [Jesus says] *"Your love* for one another will *prove* to the world that *you are my disciples."* (Emphasis added.)
>
> Ephesians 1:4–5: Even before he made the world, *God loved us and chose us in Christ* to be holy and without fault in his eyes. God decided in advance to adopt us into his own family by bringing us to himself through Jesus Christ. This is what he wanted to do, and it gave him great pleasure. (Emphasis added.)

Growing up in Christ means becoming like Christ in our character, marked by love, truth, and holiness – as was Christ's character. Wise kids make that their primary goal in their growing up years.

But God is also the source of all truth. Some of God's truth is revealed in the Bible; some is revealed in nature. As you learn what others believe, whether from books, school, Internet, TV, music, Sunday school, church, and so on, you will discover that many of these beliefs and opinions contradict each other. Those that contradict cannot all be true. Many even argue that because we all should love all people, for the sake of peace among us, we should let all people have "their own truth." But this can't be true either, because these many "personal truths" and "cultural truths" contradict each other. They should therefore be considered as opinions or beliefs. Which of these you embrace as true, should depend on the quality of the facts that are said to support the contradictory truth claims.[9]

Reflect on a few Scriptures about God being truth and so should we be.

> Joshua 22:22 The Lord, the Mighty One, is God! The Lord, the Mighty One, is *God! He knows the truth,* and may Israel know it, too! (Emphasis added.)
>
> 2 Samuel 7:28 For you are God, O Sovereign Lord. *Your words are truth,* and you have promised these good things to your servant. (Emphasis added.)
>
> **John 8:31, 32, 36** Jesus said to the people who believed in him, "You are truly my disciples if you remain *faithful to my teachings.* And *you will know the truth,* and the *truth will set you free....* So if the Son sets you free, you are *truly free."* (Emphasis added.)
>
> **John 14:17** He is the *Holy Spirit, who leads into all truth.* The world cannot receive him, because it isn't looking for him and doesn't recognize him. But you know him, because he lives with you now and later will be in you. (Emphasis added.)
>
> **John 15:26** But I will send you the *Advocate – the Spirit of truth.* He will come to you from the Father and will testify all about me. (Emphasis added.)

AT OUR HOUSE

1. **Brainstorm: How is our world messed up today?**
2. **Brainstorm: How is our world trying to clean up its messes today? How is that working?**

> **John 16:13** When the *Spirit of truth* comes, he will *guide you into all truth.* He will not speak on his own but will tell you what he has heard. He will tell you about the future. (Emphasis added.)
>
> **Ephesians 4:15** Instead, we will *speak the truth in love*, growing in every way more and more like Christ, who is the head of his body, the church. (Emphasis added.)

Wise kids want to grow up in Christ and become as truthful as He in their growing up years.

God is also infinitely holy.[10] But what does that mean? Evangelist Don Stewart writes,

> The Bible teaches that God is a holy God. The idea behind the concept of holiness is "separation." It comes from a word meaning "to separate or cut off." God is separate, or cut off, from everything that is sinful and evil – He cannot tolerate sin. John wrote this truth in figurative language. *"This is the message we have heard from him and declare to you: God is light; in him there is no darkness at all"* (1 John 1:5 NIV). To say that God is holy means there is no trace of evil in his character.[11]

Not only is God's holiness expressed in His separation *from* all evil and sin, it also shows His separation *unto* (His devotion to) all that is good and pure, as expressed in His glory or honour. God alone is infinitely good[12] and so He desires that we honour His infinite goodness as He alone possesses it. Moses saw His special presence at the burning bush in the desert. This made that ground especially holy.[13] His special presence in the tabernacle made the Holy Place especially holy and made the Most Holy Place even more holy.[14] God even commanded Israel to set

AT OUR HOUSE

1. **Where and when do you now learn about the Bible?**
2. **How much of the Bible could you now recite from memory?**
3. **How often do you reflect on (think about) what the Bible teaches about your daily life?**

apart one day each week as holy, to devote to honouring God.[15] He set apart Aaron and the priests to be utterly dedicated to wholly devoting all their energies to honouring God.[16] When Isaiah came into God's special holy presence he realized his own sin as never before by contrast.[17]

Not only is God holy, He wants us, as His children to be holy too. In 1 Peter 1:13–16 we read,

> So *prepare your minds for action* and *exercise self-control.* Put all your hope in the gracious salvation that will come to you when Jesus Christ is revealed to the world. So you must *live as God's obedient children.* Don't slip back into your old ways of living to satisfy your own desires. You didn't know any better then. But now you must *be holy in everything you do, just as God who chose you is holy.* For the Scriptures say, "*You must be holy because I am holy.*" (Emphasis added.)

Consider these Scriptures about God being holy and so should we be.

> 1 Peter 2:9*:* But you are not like that, for you are a chosen people. You are royal priests, a *holy nation,* God's very own possession. As a result, you can *show others the goodness of God,* for he called you out of the darkness into his wonderful light. (Emphasis added.)
>
> Ephesians 1:4: Even before he made the world, God loved us and *chose us in Christ to be holy and without fault in his eyes.* (Emphasis added.)
>
> Ephesians 5:25–27*:* For husbands, this means love your wives, just as Christ loved the church. He gave up his life for her to *make her holy and clean, washed by the cleansing of God's word.* He did this to present her to himself as a glorious church without a spot or wrinkle or any other blemish. Instead, *she will be holy and without fault.* (Emphasis added.)
>
> 1 John 2:1 My dear children, I am writing this to you so that you will *not sin.* But if anyone does sin, we have an advocate who pleads our case before the Father. He is Jesus Christ, the one who is *truly righteous.* (Emphasis added.)
>
> 1 John 3:2: Dear friends, we are already God's children, but he has not yet shown us what we will be like when Christ appears. But we do know that *we will be like him,* for we will see him as he really is. (Emphasis added.)

In J. C. Ryle's Christian classic, *Holiness*,[18] he writes that holiness cost Jesus His life blood, shed to atone for our sin before a just and holy God so that we could become Christians. But holiness also costs the person who decides to turn away from sin (repent) and by faith accept complete forgiveness for sin and abundant life in the Holy Spirit's power. What does it cost us? First, it costs us giving up our self-righteousness; that is, no more imagining we can be good enough on our own. Secondly, it costs us giving up our sins; that is, no more imagining we can just go on thinking and doing all the wrong things that mess up our lives and others'. Thirdly, it costs us giving up our love of ease; that is, no more imagining we can just be lazy, have naughty fun, never read or memorize the Bible or pray or share God's truth with others or help the needy. Fourthly, it costs us giving up our desire for the favour of the world; that is, no more imagining we can just go on thinking and doing all the popular things that non-Christians think and do so that we can be accepted by the non-Christians as being in the "in" crowd. Sure, we all want friends, but not those who expect us to be unloving, untruthful, or unholy. We can still love them, even if we don't pick them as our best friends.

If you really want to grow up in Christ, you will want to make choices that will develop your Christian character, especially habits of love, truth, and holiness, much like God, in whose moral image you were created, and much like Jesus who was God in human form and who revealed God to us in very understandable human ways. Clearly, some peoples' choices in our messed-up world are not loving, truthful, or holy. You will want to make it your habit to avoid these messed-up choices as much as possible. Knowing and doing what the Bible teaches are crucial. That means you will want to learn as much as you can about what the Bible teaches and how best to put it into daily practice. Also, you will want to memorize key Bible passages and learn to think about them many times a week. Perhaps you might memorize some or all the Bible texts with references printed in boldface in this book. Particularly make it a habit to think about how the Bible's teaching (for example, the passages quoted above) helps you make wise choices.

From Brook,

Some popular kids tease us, call us names, and say this "Jesus" stuff is not cool. Should I say something to them or just stay quiet?

From Uncle Al,

You might ask them, What does it mean to be "cool"? Does it mean anything more than being popular or being smart? Is it "cool" to be loved by others? Is it "cool" to love others, even those who are not popular or smart? That's what God does. Is it "cool" to believe as true what is actually true? That's what God does, because He is the source of all truth. Or is it "cool" to believe as true what is actually false? Is it really smart to do that? Or is it "cool" to behave in unholy ways? Some people say, "Yes, to be 'cool' you need to be a bit naughty sometimes." You might say, "I think it's more important to be loving, truthful, and holy like God is and the Bible teaches, than to be popular, if this means behaving in unloving, untruthful, and unholy ways." It may be fun to tease and laugh, but not at someone else's expense.

AT OUR HOUSE

1. **What does it take to be popular at your school or neighbourhood?**
2. **How important is popularity to you?**
3. **How important should popularity be to you?**

Some kids may think it's "cool" to bully others, but kids who want to grow up in Christ learn never to think that. In fact, kids who grow up in Christ are often brave enough to stand up to bullies and tell them clearly that they are being mean and uncaring about the feelings of their victims. If the bullies are too big or too many, kids in Christ sometimes prefer to get help from a responsible adult (such as a teacher, parent, or coach).

Many even argue that love requires telling lies sometimes or behaving in sinful ways sometimes. But God shows His love by being always truthful and always holy in ways we can always depend on Him. The problem with sometimes telling lies is that anyone who does that loses the trust of others. Likewise, anyone who sometimes behaves in unholy ways tends to lose the trust and respect of others. Even if their untruthful and unholy ways are lovingly motivated, that good motive does not make their wrong choices right. God never has that problem; nor should we. God can always be trusted to be loving, truthful, and holy without contradiction, and so should we.

At the heart of building positive relationships with parents, siblings, teachers, coaches, friends at school, at church, or in the community, and someday perhaps with a marriage spouse is a personal habit of always being loving, truthful, and holy. That way you will be trusted and respected by others. No relationship can endure without trust and respect. Sure, we all mess up sometimes, but when we do, we need to apologize and seek to rebuild positive relationships with others by demonstrating personal habits of being loving, truthful, and holy always. God makes love, truth, and holiness work, and so should we. That's an important part of growing up in Christ.

One way to prove our love to others is to tell the truth about sin, both ours and theirs, in order to tell them truthfully and lovingly the good news of the forgiveness of sin and the salvation (rescue) from sin's power and penalty that Christ provided through His atoning death for us on the cross of Calvary. Those times might be some of the most joyful times you'll experience

AT OUR HOUSE

1. **What does it mean for us to be "holy"?**
2. **Study 1 Peter 1:13–25 in NIV or NLT.**
3. **How do love, truth and being holy relate to each other in this passage?**

in your life; though they might be some of the most stressful times, depending on how others respond to your telling them this good news. Warning others lovingly of the dangers toward which they are moving is not always fun, especially if they respond badly. But if they respond by turning around and accepting Christ's free gift of forgiveness for sin, this can be a most joyful experience and help build strong positive relationships. Silence in the presence of danger may be more cowardly than loving, regardless of popular contrary opinions today in our messed-up world. "In a time of deceit, telling the truth becomes a revolutionary act."[19] How about this motto: "Love God, Love People, Do Something About It!"[20]

If some people tell you that there is no God or that the Bible cannot be trusted to tell us the truth, you can simply ask them why they think they are right about that. Ask them, Why does anything at all exist?[21] Ask them how they think our huge beautiful universe came to be here now.[22] Surely our universe did not create itself – that's not possible. Ask them how they think living things came to be here now. All living things we see were brought into existence by other living things. If someone wants to imagine that our universe and life just somehow magically popped into existence for no reason at all, they are free to imagine such ideas, but that does not make them true. Ask them how they think humans came to be so sure that some behaviours are absolutely wrong morally and other behaviours are absolutely right morally. On many moral issues humans have agreed throughout history and around the world in every culture. The Bible tells us much about that. Sure, some people have differing beliefs about such questions, and we should love and respect them as people also made in God's image, but differing beliefs do not show that all of them are false. You might also look in *Dealing with Doubts and Differences* (Book Four in the *Growing Up In Christ* series) for further discussions of such issues.

2 PUBERTY FOR GIRLS AND BOYS

Hi, Brook and Ryan,

Let's talk about how your body and mind will be changing during your "tween" years (ages 8–12) and teen years (ages 13–19) as you grow up from being a child to becoming the young woman or young man God has designed you to be. Depending on the attitudes you choose, the changes in your body and mind known as "puberty" may be some of the most exciting and challenging stages of your life. Because you can choose your attitudes and reactions, some of these changes you can control. Others you can't. Puberty is all about growing up from an older child into a young woman or young man! Depending on how you choose in those areas which you can control, you will either grow up in Christ, which is what you, your parents and God want for you, or you may grow up messed-up or broken, as too many kids do these days.

Among those areas you cannot control are how you are growing smarter and stronger. But you can choose whether you exercise your intelligence and muscles diligently or whether you will be mentally, spiritually, or physically lazy. You can choose whether or not you learn healthy eating, recreation, thinking, and sleeping habits.

Another area you cannot control is your rapid growth. That happens at different ages and in varying amounts among girls and boys your age. Longer legs and arms can make kids awkward and stumbling at times – nothing to worry about. A good sense of humour helps. A healthy confidence that you can handle life's stresses is important. Don't let anyone humiliate you when embarrassing accidents happen to you. And make sure you never humiliate anyone else when embarrassing accidents happen to them. Learn to practise friendly humour, not bullying.

Stretching muscles can give you "growing pains." The genes you inherited from your parents help decide your size, shape, bones and muscles, eye colour, skin issues, and hair texture, even whether you will have freckles. But you did not choose your parents, so why should anyone bully you over what is simply not your choice?

When God created the world and everything good in it, He designed all living things to reproduce "after their kind." Almost all living things are reproduced by having a male sperm join a female egg to cause a new offspring to start to grow. That's what happened when your dad's sperm joined your mom's egg (ovum) and you were conceived in your mom's tummy. As you began to grow in your mom's tummy long before you were born, God gave you special reproductive organs so that when you are all grown up and perhaps marry, you too could conceive babies. Before you go through puberty your reproductive organs are not ready to conceive a baby because you are not yet a young woman or man. (Notice that the "Glossary/Words to Know" near the back of this book defines the medical terms and indicates how to pronounce them correctly.)

All the billions of adult women and men around the world now and throughout human history went through puberty (except Adam and Eve, who were created as adults). So did your mom and dad. Your "tween" years are very important to get ready for these necessary changes, especially because you really can't know exactly when these changes will begin or how long they will take. Each person is unique. God has designed puberty as a one- to two-year burst of changes in your body, especially your brain and sex organs, that biologically enable girls to become moms and boys to become dads. Most girls begin puberty around ages 9½ to 12, but a very few begin as early as age 8 and a very few begin as late as age 16. Most girls finish puberty around ages 13 to 15, but a very few finish as early as age 11 and a very few finish as late as age 21. Most boys begin puberty a year or two later, around ages 10 to 13, but a very few begin as early as age 9 and a very few begin as late as age 16. Most boys finish puberty around ages 15 to 17, but a very few finish as early as age 14 and a very few finish as late as age 20, when they start growing a beard. Your brain will likely not be full grown till you are about age 25. You need the confidence that God is never too early or too late and that every girl and boy becomes a physically mature woman or man at the right time.

It seems that over 90 percent of kids struggle with acne at some time during puberty. Acne is a normal, but often frustrating, skin condition described as follows at the Kids Health website:

> Acne is the name for those red bumps called pimples that a lot of kids and teens get on their skin. When your skin's oil glands make too much oil, the tiny holes on your skin called pores get stopped up with oil, dead skin, and bacteria. Then the skin around these clogged pores can swell and look lumpy or red. Usually, this happens during puberty, when your body is changing from a kid into an adult.[23]

Washing at least twice a day with lots of soap can help. Some skin creams available at drug stores can also help clear your skin. Usually they take several months to clear your skin. You'll likely have smooth skin when you finish puberty, so try not to get too upset while this is happening.

Many emotional and mental changes happen at the same time. For example, some girls who were never interested in boys suddenly get very interested in boys, often in boys older than they are. Similarly, some boys for whom girls were mostly a bother may suddenly notice girls as never before, especially girls who have recently "filled out" in more womanly shapes.

In 1 Timothy 4:12 (NIV) God instructs young Christians: Don't let anyone look down on you because you are young, but set an example for the believers in speech, in conduct, in love, in faith and in purity.

Since we live in a messed-up world, girls and boys who begin or finish puberty early or late can get quite embarrassed about that and can get teased and bullied by others about it. Kids who want to grow up in Christ make sure that they never bully others about anything. They learn to love and respect everyone as created in God's image.[24] As caring bystanders they even stand up for others they see being bullied, telling a parent, teacher, school counsellor, or authority figure about what is happening. Not doing so may be as bad as bullying. Someone has wisely said, "The way that people treat you is a statement about who they are as a human being. It is not a statement about you."[25]

In recent years social media have become a significant part of the lives of many kids who have web access. Sadly, too many kids have become victims of cyberbullying. Kids who want to grow up in Christ may want to take the "Be Love" pledge which reads as follows:

We promise to
1. Harness the Positive Power of Social Media
2. Treat Others the Way We Want to Be Treated
3. Type With Care and Think Before We Send
4. Build a Web of Respect and an Online Community of Trust[26]

AT OUR HOUSE

1. **Ask your mom and dad what they recall of their puberty ups and downs.**
2. **Ask your mom and dad if they were bullied as kids, and what they did about it.**
3. **Ask your mom and dad how they dealt with issues of love, truth, and being holy.**

From Ryan,

What starts these puberty changes, and what are the first signs?

From Uncle Al,

God has designed hormones (special chemicals produced by the pituitary gland at the bottom of your brain) to trigger the development of male and female sex characteristics as boys and girls become men and women. Sometimes the first sign of puberty is the growth of hair in the armpits, legs, and pubic areas (above the boy's penis and the girl's vulva). Sometimes the first sign is a sudden growth spurt, including longer legs and arms for boys and girls, and wider hips for girls. Most boys and girls beginning puberty produce new body odours, especially if they don't shower or bathe daily. Thoroughly washing your genitals and pubic areas with soap daily becomes more important at this time of your life.

Sometimes the first signs of puberty are the mental abilities and interests to understand more abstract ideas and relationships, such as courage, loyalty, and long-term consequences for attitudes and choices. Children think in more concrete terms of things they can see. Adults add to this the ability to think in abstract terms, like character, worthy goals, and delaying the filling of desires. Both abstract and concrete thinking are needed if you want to grow up in Christ.

Boys' voices also change during puberty.

The next two chapters provide more detailed discussions of girls' and boys' reproductive organs, their developments at puberty, their functions in a wholesome marriage, and their emotional and relational dimensions. Girls and boys who really want to grow up in Christ need to understand these according to God's loving, truthful, and holy design. How girls' reproductive organs change during puberty is the focus of Chapter 3. How boys' reproductive organs change during puberty is the focus of Chapter 4.

Puberty is also the time when most girls and boys first experience sexual arousal. What prompts sexual arousal can vary widely among girls and boys, including private fantasies with no other person present, looking at an attractive member of the opposite sex (or pictures of them on TV, in movies, on the Internet, and so on), or simple or passionate kissing, caressing, and other touching.

In Chapters 5 to 7 the focus is on how girls and boys need to grow up healthy in these important areas. Then in Chapters 8 to 11 the focus is on our need to understand something of how sinful humans have messed up in these areas, so that you can understand something of how to avoid some dangerous mistakes that others around you may be making. You also need to commit to loving and respecting others as created in God's image, regardless of what mistakes they may be making.

3 PUBERTY FOR GIRLS

Hi, Brook,

Ms. Barb here. You've been taught that God has designed your body as a precious gift to you. Right?

Let's talk about how your body and mind will be changing during your tween and teen years as you grow up to be the woman God has designed you to become.

When God created the world and everything good in it, He designed all living things to reproduce "after their kind." Almost all living things are reproduced by having a male sperm join a female egg to cause a new offspring to start to grow. That's what happened when your dad's sperm joined your mom's egg (ovum) and she conceived a baby (you). As you began to grow in your mom's uterus long before you were born, God gave you special reproductive organs so that when you are all grown up and marry your husband, together you too might conceive a baby in your tummy. Before you go through puberty, your reproductive organs are not ready to conceive a baby because you are not yet a young woman.

Except for Adam and Eve, all adult men and women have gone through puberty. Your tween years are very important to get ready for these necessary changes, especially because you really can't know exactly when these changes will begin or how long they will take.

Each person is unique.

Let's explore the parts that allow you to become a mother someday, after you marry. To protect your body, it's best that you allow only your parents (when you are young), a doctor, and your husband (after you are married) to see and touch these private parts (though other girls might see them at a group shower in a gym or swimming pool). Breasts may be the first to develop as you enter puberty, but not always. By God's design, breasts are mostly fat mixed with glands that can produce milk after a baby is born. You can't see these glands because they are inside the breast, but they have ducts, or vessels, that attach to a nipple, the darker-coloured part of a breast. These nipples are what babies' mouths attach to so they can get the milk. That's called nursing. You may want to have your mom help you shop for your first bra so that your nipples can't be seen through your clothing, and to make sure it's a comfortable fit, especially if you play sports or do vigorous exercise.

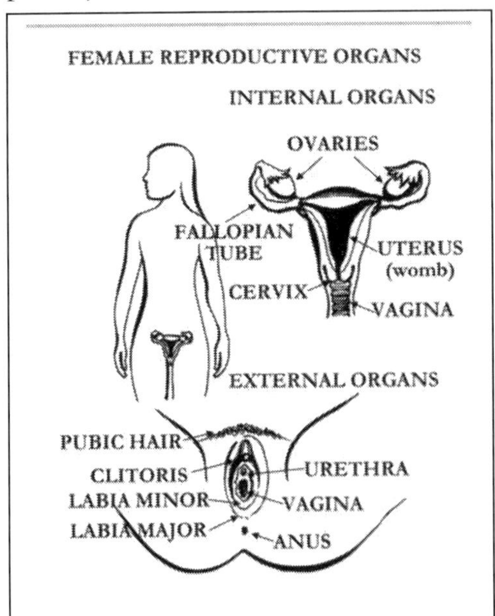

In the diagram, notice that the abdominal reproductive parts are in two groups: the external and internal groups. The external parts are designed to guard the internal parts against infection and to allow your husband's sperm to enter your internal parts. They include the vulva[†] (where your pubic hair grows when you start puberty) and the major and minor labia (skin folds that cover the clitoris and openings of the urethra and vagina). The clitoris is a pea-sized organ that has a

[†] Note the definitions of medical terms in the Glossary/ Words to Know near the end of this book.

role in your future sexual arousal (an excitement expecting sexual activity). The urethra is the channel through which you can drain urine from your bladder ("pee"). The vagina is the channel through which you will likely deliver your babies, if you become a mom. God has designed you so that when you get specially aroused sexually, the vagina will get wet, ready to receive a male penis.

Note that your anus is not a sexual organ (that is, it is not part of your reproductive organs). It's simply designed to eliminate your solid wastes (called "stool" or "poop") at the end of your digestive system. The key caution here is to wipe this area from front to back after every bowel movement so as to avoid infections in your genitals (reproductive organs, especially external sex organs).

When you were born, your ovaries already contained thousands of tiny partly formed eggs (called "ova" [plural], each being an "ovum" [singular]). During puberty, your ovaries begin to produce estrogen, a hormone that controls your puberty development. After puberty, normally about once a month at ovulation, one ovum will mature enough to move through one fallopian tube to your uterus (womb), which has produced a lining to cushion the fertilized ovum or egg. That happens in all adult women. Once, when it happened in your mom, your dad's sperm met your mom's ovum (egg cell) and fertilized it so that you started to grow as a new baby; that is, you were "conceived." That's very exciting! That's how God beautifully designed this part of your body called reproductive organs. That's when your life began! But it took a few weeks before your mom knew that she was pregnant with you. By that time, likely your heart was already pumping blood through your tiny growing body about the size of a bean (about three to four weeks after you were conceived).

When you are married, when you and your husband "make love" (or have sexual intercourse) as God designed that you should, you too may conceive a baby. When you get sexually aroused, your vagina (a three- to four-inch tube of stretchy muscle) will expand and lubricate itself so that intercourse will be easier and more pleasant for you. When your husband ejaculates, his sperm will move up your vagina, through your cervix and perhaps fertilize an ovum in your uterus. Normally about nine months later your baby will have grown enough to be born into our world. This will give you great joy to be a new mom! This is all God's wonderful invention. Your growing family will give you and your husband many gloriously happy times and some serious challenges as you go through life together. You'll want your kids to grow up in Christ and healthy too.

Of course, most of your ova will not get fertilized. (You don't want to give birth to hundreds of kids!) If the ovum does not get fertilized, the lining that was formed inside the uterus is expelled through your vagina once a month. It looks like blood. This is called menses or menstruation or a period. For most girls the menstrual flow (about two tablespoons or 30 ml) will finish in about three to seven days. You'll want to chat with your mom about the best way to catch the menstrual tissues and blood with a pad or a tampon and how to have extras with you at the appropriate times. Also chat with your mom about the best way to deal with the little cramping (like a muscle spasm that moves the material through the vagina) and your mood changes at those times. At first your periods may be irregular, but soon they will become a more regular monthly cycle. It helps to keep a record of when you have your periods.

Some girls in puberty think a lot about boys, perhaps even of one in particular. Others don't. Both are normal. An adult body has about 50 different hormones.[27] Some people suggest that no two people are the same in how their hormones influence them. Hormones should not cause you any anxieties. Patience is the most important virtue at this time. You can grow up in Christ and healthy if your values are biblical. It is very important to discuss your confusions and feelings with your parents at this time.

Some girls discover that touching or rubbing their genitals can give them pleasant feelings. Such discoveries can be quite innocent. But if they lead to imagining having sexual intercourse with a man, they can become an unhealthy obsession, especially if the masturbating girls add the stimulus of looking at pictures or videos of attractive men. Pornography is so readily available on the Internet that staying away from such unhealthy obsessions is vital to helping you grow up in Christ and healthy. See further discussion of this in Chapter 9.

Remember that each girl and each boy goes through puberty at their own unique time and rate. Also girls tend to go through their puberty a year or two earlier than boys do. Hence, during puberty girls are often taller than boys their own age. There is no good reason for any teasing or bullying over such differences. Most boys eventually tend to grow taller than girls their own age. Take moral courage: All girls and boys grow into normal women and men after they finish their own unique puberty. Take a positive attitude, perhaps even a sense of humour, to the entire process.

Girls and boys both bully by calling their victims insulting names or physically pushing them around in rude and mean ways. Some bullies exclude their victims from social events relationships and more. Some spread false rumours about their victims. Some simply fail to protect and care for weaker or vulnerable people, such as the sick, the poor, the elderly, the mentally ill or handicapped, as well as

AT OUR HOUSE

1. **Brook, ask your mom about shopping for bras and the best way to handle your periods.**
2. **Brook, ask your mom if she wants to tell you anything about how you were conceived as an overflow of her love for your dad.**
3. **Brook, ask your mom about how the love she and your dad share reflects the love, truth, and holiness that God the Father, Son, and Holy Spirit share.**

BONUS: Visit a doctor's office or museum that has life-sized models of babies growing from conception to birth.

children.

Bullying is always a way of showing that the bully would rather hurt others than show them the love and respect they deserve as people made in God's image, regardless of what they believe, say, or do. Girls who want to grow up in Christ will always resist the temptation to bully others. Instead, they will practise the brave moral courage that it takes to stand up to bullies. This can sometimes be risky, especially if the bullies are bigger and stronger than you are. In that case you need to get help, for the sake of the mistreated victims. Part of growing up to be an in-Christ woman is learning to protect and care for weaker or vulnerable people such as the sick, the poor, the elderly, the mentally ill or handicapped, as well as your husband and children.

On the whole, you are likely to find that growing up through your tween and teen years may be one of the most exciting adventures of your life, especially if you make wise choices about your physical, mental, spiritual, and relational health.

From Brook,

My friend has no mom. She's growing up in a home with just a dad. I have another friend who has no mom and is growing up in a home with two dads. How can I help them with these issues?

From Ms. Barb,

You raise an important challenge in our culture and one that seems to be getting bigger every year. Some moms die before their kids are grown and their dads don't remarry very soon or ever. Some parents divorce, and kids live with their dads, whether one or more. No dad can really be a mom to his kids, no matter how hard he may try. We live in a messed-up world, and kids in such challenging homes need our love, respect, and help.

You could suggest that such motherless girls read this chapter, perhaps even this whole book. You could suggest they join you for Sunday school, kids' clubs at church, sports, camp or other activities where they might get to know other moms who could help them sort out the questions you discuss from time to time with your mom. Some motherless girls can find some motherly help, answers' and encouragement from a motherly neighbour, grandma, aunt, coach, teacher' or older friend. Perhaps you might be that friend.

4 PUBERTY FOR BOYS

Hi Ryan,

Uncle Al here. You've been taught that God has designed your body as a precious gift to you. Right?

Let's talk about how your body and mind will be changing during your tween and teen years as you grow up to be the man God has designed you to become. A changing voice may sometime mess up your speech. That will soon clear up as you settle into your more manly speaking and singing voice.

When God created the world and everything good in it, He designed all living things to reproduce "after their kind." Almost all living things are reproduced by having a male sperm join a female egg to cause a new offspring to start to grow. That's what happened when your dad's sperm joined your mom's egg (ovum) and you were conceived. As you began to grow in your mom's uterus long before you were born, God gave you special reproductive organs so that when you are all grown up and marry your wife, together you too might conceive a baby. Before you go through puberty your reproductive organs are not ready to conceive a baby because you are not yet a young man.

But all adult men and women went through puberty (except Adam and Eve, who were created as adults). Your tween years are very important to get ready for these necessary changes, especially because you really can't know exactly when these changes will begin or how long they will take. Each person is unique. Most boys begin puberty around ages 12 to 14, but a very few begin as early as age 10 and a very few begin as late as age 16. Most boys finish puberty around ages 15 to 17, but a very few finish as early as age 14 and a very few finish as late as age 21. Your brain will likely not be full grown till you are about age 25.

Puberty begins when your pituitary gland (at the bottom of your brain) releases certain hormones that prompt your testicles ("balls") to grow bigger and release another hormone called testosterone, which starts to grow hair under your arms, on your face, and in your pubic area above your penis. When you grow facial hair (in a moustache and beard form), you might ask your dad how best to deal with this new development.

Since we live in a messed-up world, boys and girls who begin or finish puberty early or late can get quite embarrassed about it and can get teased and bullied. Kids who want to grow up in Christ and healthy make sure that they never bully others about anything. They even stand up for others who they see being bullied.

Because boys usually grow to be a bit bigger and stronger than the girls, it seems that boys like to show off their muscles and toughness more. This leads some boys to more readily want to bully others, especially those they see as being smaller or weaker. Whether this is by calling their victims insulting names or physically pushing them around in rude and mean ways, bullying is always a way of showing that the bully would rather hurt others than show them the love and respect they deserve as people made in God's image, regardless of what they believe, say, or do. Boys who want to grow up in Christ will always resist the temptation to bully others. Instead, they will practise the brave moral courage that it takes to stand up to bullies. This can sometimes be risky, especially if the bullies are bigger and stronger than you are. In that case you need to get help, for the sake of the mistreated victims. Part of growing up to be a gentleman is learning to protect and care for weaker or vulnerable people such as the sick, the poor, the elderly, the mentally ill or handicapped, as well as your wife and children. This may also become part of your teaching the bullies that they too need to grow up to be gentlemen, to protect and care for weaker or vulnerable people. You might even challenge the bullies to realize that they only bully those they see as smaller or weaker than they are. That is a glaring example of their lack of empathy for others. It's also a glaring example of their own cowardice – hardly a manly trait!

Let's explore your reproductive body parts because God designed them as His precious gifts to you, so that, if all goes well, you can become a dad when you marry. To keep safe it's best to let only your parents (when you are young), a doctor, and your wife (after you are married) see and touch these (though other boys might see them at a group shower in a gym or swimming pool).

In the diagram, notice how your reproductive parts are all in your lower abdominal area. Your main sex organs are your penis[†] and testicles. Your testicles are the two glands in your scrotum (the loose-skinned bag behind your penis). These produce about 100 million sperm daily, designed to fertilize your wife's ova when you are married. God has designed your penis with a shaft (the longest part), a glans (the specially shaped head) and the foreskin (the loose skin that covers the glans, unless you have been circumcised at birth). God has designed your penis to serve two very

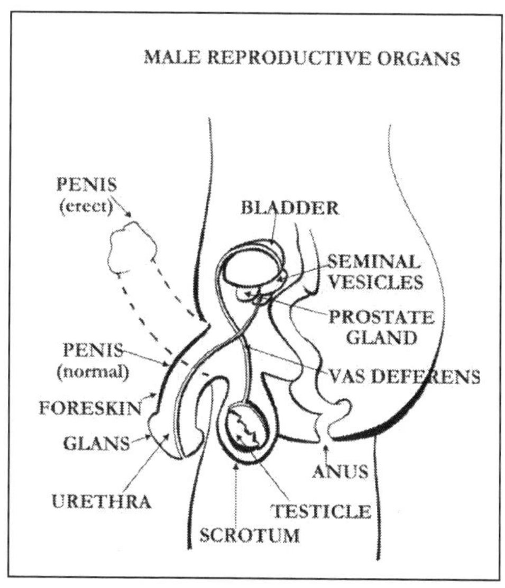

[†] Note the definitions of medical terms in the Glossary/Words to Know near the end of this book.

different functions. All your life you have been using it for passing your urine ("peeing"). The bladder collects your urine (liquid waste) from your body, and the prostate releases it through your urethra when you pee. But when you are grown up and married you will also use it very differently when you and your wife "make love" (have sexual intercourse) as God designed that you should. At such times your penis will get sexually aroused into a hard erect state, so that it can penetrate your wife's vagina, and at your euphoric climax it will ejaculate semen (a cream-coloured fluid produced by your seminal vesicles), filled with between two and six hundred million sperm from your testicles. This is a precious life-giving gift that God has designed you to give only to your wife. If the time is right in your wife's cycle, one sperm may fertilize an ovum and your baby will be conceived. This is all very exciting! That's how God beautifully designed human reproductive organs. This is all God's wonderful invention. Your growing family will give you and your wife many gloriously happy times and some serious challenges as you go through life together. You'll want your kids to grow up in Christ and healthy too.

A key factor is that during sexual intercourse your prostate gland will close off your bladder and open up the duct ("vas deferens") from your testicles so that only semen from your seminal vesicles and sperm from your testicles will flow through your urethra.

A normal but sometimes troubling event is that during your puberty, at any time, day or night, your penis may fill with blood and stand erect, ready for sexual intercourse. This can happen several times in one day, or not at all. It can be embarrassing if it happens during the day, but it's not your fault. You might ask your dad how to deal with such situations. If this happens at night, your penis may even ejaculate some semen into your pyjamas and bed in what is commonly called a "wet dream," whether or not you were having a sexy dream at the time. Again, it's not your fault, so there is no need to feel guilty. It's best to get such soiled pyjamas and bed sheets washed as soon as possible with minimal embarrassment. Such events are simply signs that you are growing up to be a man.

Extra careful daily washing of your penis and scrotum are important to maintain good health. Note that your anus is not a sexual organ (that is, it is not part of your reproductive organs). It's simply designed to eliminate your solid wastes (called "stool" or "poop") at the end of your digestive system. The key caution here is to wipe this area from front to back after every bowel movement so as to avoid infections in your genitals.

At some time during puberty your voice will change to lower notes. This can also bring embarrassment, if your voice sometimes "cracks" from its higher child range to its lower manly range. It may help if you laugh this off (such as calling these events your attempts at yodelling).

Some boys in puberty think a lot about girls, perhaps even of one in particular. Others don't. Both are normal. About 50 different hormones are at work in an adult body.[28] Some people suggest that no two people are the same in how their different hormones influence them. Hormones should not cause you any anxieties. Patience is the most important virtue at this time. You can grow up in Christ and healthy, if your values are biblical. It is very important to discuss your confusions and feelings with your parents at this time.

Some boys discover that touching or rubbing their genitals can give them pleasant feelings. Such discoveries can be quite innocent. But if they lead to imagining having sexual intercourse with a woman, they can become an unhealthy obsession, especially if the masturbating boys add the stimulus of looking at pictures or videos of attractive women. Pornography is so readily available on the Internet that staying away from such unhealthy obsessions is vital to helping you grow up in Christ and healthy. See further discussion of this in Chapter 9.

Remember that each boy and each girl goes through puberty at their own unique time and rate. Also girls tend to go through their puberty a year or two earlier than boys do. Hence, during puberty girls are often taller than boys their own age. There is no good reason for any teasing or bullying over such differences. Most boys eventually tend to grow taller than girls their own age. Take moral courage: All boys and girls grow into normal men and women after they finish their own unique puberty. Take a positive attitude, perhaps even a sense of humour, to the entire process.

On the whole, you are likely to find that growing up through your tween and teen years may be one of the most exciting adventures of your life, especially if you make wise choices about your physical, mental, spiritual, and relational health.

From Ryan,

My friend has no dad. He's growing up in a home with just a mom. I have another friend who has no dad and is growing up in a home with two moms. How can I help them with these issues?

From Uncle Al,

These kids face an important challenge and one that seems to be growing bigger every year. Some dads die before their kids are grown and their moms don't remarry very soon or ever. Some parents divorce, and kids grow up with their moms, whether one or more. No mom can really be a dad to her kids, no matter how hard she may try. We live in a messed-up world and kids in such challenging homes need our love, respect and help.

You could suggest that such fatherless boys and girls read this chapter, perhaps even this whole book. You could suggest they join you for Sunday school, kids' clubs at church, kids' sports, camp, or other activities where they might get to know other dads who could help them sort out the questions you discuss from time to time with your dad. Some fatherless boys and girls can find some fatherly help, answers and encouragement from a fatherly neighbour, grandpa, uncle, coach, teacher, or older friend. Perhaps you might be that friend.

5 AIM TO BE WHOLE

Hi, Brook and Ryan,

As you grow up to become a mature Christian woman or man, you'll want to make every choice toward the goal of becoming as whole as God intended you to be. "What does that mean?" you ask. It means you clearly understand a few basic principles of the Christian life and make them a habitual part of your daily life. It means you want to think, believe, and do what God knows is right, regardless of how others in our messed-up world think, believe, and do differently. It means you want to embrace as your own what God describes as a truly Christian goal of your life, pattern of life, motive of life, and power of the Christian life. Of course this all begins with a clear commitment to being a born-again Christian. That includes repenting of (turning away from) your sin and by faith accepting God's free gift of forgiveness and a new life in Christ.[29]

The goal of the Christian life is to glorify God

Have you noticed how most people in our messed-up world think that the purpose of life is to satisfy themselves?[30] So they pursue goals such as fun and pleasure, money and possessions, popularity and fame, reputation and power, new experiences and knowledge, drugs and alcohol, sex and relationships, and so on. Have you noticed that none of these goals are satisfying in the long-run, even if they may give people short-term thrills and satisfaction?

The Bible gives us a much more satisfying life goal: to glorify God. He created us in His image[31] and redeemed us from our sin so that we should grow to be like Him. In 1 Corinthians 10:31 Paul writes: So whether you eat or drink, or whatever you do, do it *all for the glory of God.* (Emphasis added.) In Ephesians 1:12–14 Paul writes,

> *God's purpose was_*that we Jews who were the first to trust in Christ would *bring praise and glory to God.* And now you Gentiles have also heard the truth, the Good News that God saves you. And when you believed in Christ, he identified you as his own by giving you the Holy Spirit, whom he promised long ago. The Spirit is God's guarantee that he will give us the inheritance he promised and that he has purchased us to be his own people. *He did this so we would praise and glorify him.* (Emphasis added.)

In Romans 15:6 Paul writes, Then all of you can join together with one voice, *giving praise and glory to God,* the Father of our Lord Jesus Christ. (Emphasis added.)

In Jesus' Sermon on the Mount He tells us why we should be salt and light in our dark world: In the same way, let your good deeds shine out for all to see, *so that everyone will praise your heavenly Father* (Matthew 5:16, emphasis added.). Then He adds: But you are to be *perfect,* even as your Father in heaven is *perfect* (Matthew 5:48, emphasis added.).

From Ryan,

Did you say that we are to praise and glorify God by being "perfect"? But that's impossible in this life, isn't it?

From Uncle Al,

You're right, Ryan. Still, God sets that out as our goal for moral and spiritual growth. In Philippians 3:12–14 (NIV) Paul writes,

> Not that I have already obtained all this, or have already arrived at my goal, but I press on to take hold of that for which Christ Jesus took hold of me. Brothers and sisters, I do not consider myself yet to have taken hold of it. But one thing I do: Forgetting what is behind and straining toward what is ahead, *I press on toward the goal* to win the prize for which God has called me heavenward in Christ Jesus. (Emphasis added.)

The Greek word for "perfect" in Matthew 5:48 is *teleios.* It occurs 19 times in the New Testament in 17 verses. It means "brought to its end, finished, wanting nothing necessary to completeness, perfect, that which is perfect, consummate human integrity and virtue, of men: full grown, adult, of full age, mature."[32] In other words, *teleios* means to become "whole" as we use that term in this *Growing up in Christ* series. Paul writes further: So we tell others about Christ, warning everyone and teaching everyone with all the wisdom God has given us. We want to present them to God, *perfect* in their relationship to Christ (Colossians 1:28, emphasis added.). Just a few verses earlier (vs. 22, 23) he said,

> Yet now he has reconciled you to himself through the death of Christ in his physical body. As a result, he has brought you into his own presence, and you are *holy* and *blameless* as you stand before him *without a single fault*. But you must continue to believe this *truth* and *stand firmly* in it. Don't drift away from the *assurance* you received when you heard the *Good News*._(Emphasis added.)

The Epistle to the Hebrews closes with a benediction that includes this: Now may the God of peace ... equip you with *all you need for doing his will*. May he produce in you, through the power of Jesus Christ, every good thing that is pleasing to him. *All glory to him* forever and ever! Amen (13:20–21, emphasis added.). You may have heard this in church many times at the benediction.

From Brook,

Exactly how are we to "glorify God?"

From Ms. Barb,

In the world around us, we glorify or honour people, leaders, teachers, coaches, heroes, sports stars, and movie stars by our speech. We tell others how great they are and what we like about them. When we glorify God, we do more than that. We demonstrate what our God is like, showing people who we are by what we say and do and how we say or do everything. Just as an electric wire is a conduit of the power flowing through it, we are to be a conduit of Jesus to the world, allowing Him to flow through us to the people we meet every day.

Paul uses an interesting visual aid to help us understand this. He writes in 2 Corinthians 3:18, So all of us who have had that veil removed can see and *reflect the glory of the Lord.* And the Lord – who is the Spirit – *makes us more and more like him as we are changed into his glorious image.* (Emphasis added.) Paul tells us to grow in our Christian life as mirrors of God's glorious character, always reflecting more perfectly who God is. In other words, growing up to be whole means we should always aim toward becoming more loving, truthful, and holy like God already is perfectly. That's a tall order. Still that's to be our life goal. Every moral and spiritual choice we make should bring us closer to that goal.

Of course, the mirrors we use daily tell us nothing about our character, or who we are on the inside – the part that God cares about. They show only what we look like physically. It seems that's all that some people care about. Their wants and desires come before what God wants for them. But then, that's because they have their priorities messed up. God cares about our spiritual growth, how we are learning to think like He does and act like He wants us to so we stay away from things that might hurt us in the future. He helps us change "into His glorious image" more and more when we say "yes" to Him, placing our own selfish desires under His control (die to self), and follow Him no matter where that leads (take up our cross and follow Him).[33] God has given us the perfect visual aid to help us understand what He is like by sending His Son to earth to reveal to us what His glorious image is like on our planet. Paul tells us that everything works together toward this goal. In Romans 8:28–29 he writes, And we know that God causes everything to work together for the good of those who love God and are called according to his purpose for them. For God knew his people in advance, and he chose them *to become like his Son,* so that his Son would be the firstborn among many brothers and sisters. (Emphasis added.) That's really the point of the slogan "What Would Jesus Do?"

Paul writes in 1 Corinthians 6:19–20 Don't you realize that your body is the temple of the Holy Spirit, who lives in you and was given to you by

God? You do not belong to yourself, for God bought you with a high price. So you must *honor God with your body.* (Emphasis added.) This was also the goal of Jesus' life. Philippians 2:9–11 reads, Therefore, God elevated him to the place of highest honor and gave him the name above all other names, that at the name of Jesus every knee should bow, in heaven and on earth and under the earth, and every tongue declare that Jesus Christ is Lord, *to the glory of God* the Father. (Emphasis added.)

God makes love, truth, and holiness work in everything He does – so did Jesus and so should we. The goal of the Christian life is to glorify God, and one way to do that is to become like Christ. Now, that's really growing up to be whole!

The patterns of the Christian life are primarily Scripture and Christ, secondarily natural law

In the Bible God makes very clear by what behaviour patterns we too should make love, truth, and holiness work in our lives. For example in Exodus 20:1–17 He lists His Ten Commandments.

From Ryan,

Some kids say we don't live in Old Testament times anymore, so that's not for us these days. Is that right?

From Uncle Al,

That's partly right. Since Jesus came and died for us, we no longer need to do the temple sacrifices they did back then. Hebrews explains how Israel's ceremonial law was fulfilled by Christ. Also, many Old Testament civil laws were to direct how Israel was to run as a new nation in Canaan. Today we don't live in that nation. But much of the Old Testament's moral teaching was part of how God wants His people to behave. That part is called the "moral law" and that applies today as much as ever. That includes the Ten Commandments in Exodus and Jesus' Sermon on the Mount.

Here's a brief kids' summary of the Ten Commandments:

1. *Love God more than anything else.*
2. *Make nothing more important to you than God.*
3. *Use God's name only with love and respect.*

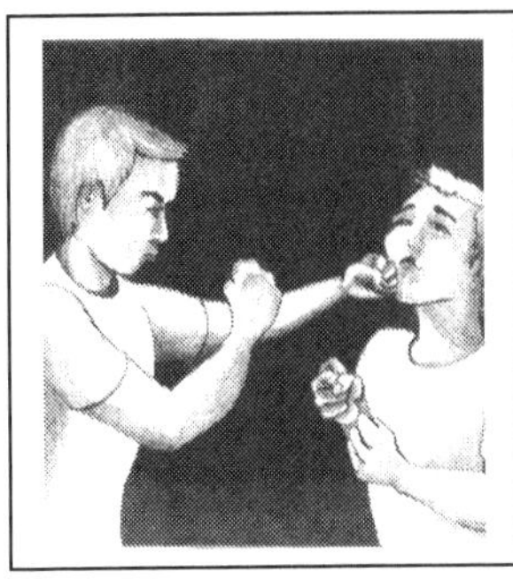

4. *Respect God's Sabbath as holy.*
5. *Love and obey your parents.*
6. *Never murder anyone.*
7. *Keep your marriage vows.*
8. *Never take what's not yours.*
9. *Never lie; always tell the truth.*
10. *Never envy others or covet things or relationships; be content with what you have.*

The most famous preacher in world history was Jesus. His most famous sermon was the Sermon on the Mount (Matthew 5 to 7). Here Jesus explains what God's moral law means and how we need to be whole as God wants us to be, not like hypocritical religious teachers (Matthew 5:20). He also shows six times how hypocritical religious teachers have misunderstood the Bible. Here Jesus shows us how compassionate He was and how well He could debate false beliefs. In the Beatitudes (Matthew 5:3–12) Jesus explains God's views of true happiness. In 5:13–16 He talks about our influence as salt (to add taste and stop disease in our world) and to add light (to show truth and holiness in our dark world – as Saint Francis of Assisi said, "All the darkness in the world cannot extinguish the light cast by a single candle"[34]). In 5:17–19 He affirms His complete faith in Scripture. In 5:21–26 Jesus explains that in God's view our being angry with someone and murdering that person can both be sinful. In 5:27–28 Jesus explains that in God's view, our imagining having sex with someone to whom we are not married and actually having sex with that person are both sinful. In 5:31–32 He shows how wrong divorce is. In 5:33–37 He explains how we must always tell the truth, even without vows. In 5:38–48 He explains how we must never take revenge, but always love our enemies. In 5:48 He declares, You are to be perfect *[teleios]*, even as your Father in heaven is perfect (as we already saw above).

In Matthew 6:1–18 Jesus teaches us how to give to needy people, how to pray (including the Lord's Prayer), and how to fast. In 6:19–34 He teaches us a wholesome attitude to money and how not to worry. In 7:1–6 Jesus teaches about judging. In 7:7–11 He teaches more about prayer. In 7:12 Jesus gives us the "Golden Rule" – Do to others whatever you would like them to do to you. In 7:13–23 He teaches about true and false disciples. He concludes this classic sermon in 7:24–29 by contrasting someone who actually follows His teaching (like a wise builder on rock) with someone who doesn't (like a foolish builder on sand). That's why this book argues that kids who make the right choices grow up to be whole, and those who don't, get messed up.

The rest of the New Testament includes many other eternal principles of how we should reflect God's infinite glory, particularly His infinite love, truth, and holiness. One such is the "fruit of the Spirit" in Galatians 5:22–23: But the Holy Spirit produces this kind of fruit in our lives: love, joy, peace, patience, kindness, goodness, faithfulness, gentleness, and self-control. There is no law against these things! Some consider this as a character sketch of Jesus, into whose likeness we are to grow.

God's moral law is also revealed in how He has created our universe, including our bodies and minds.[35] For example we don't need a Bible verse to tell us not to jump out of 10th-storey windows or not to take mind-bending drugs that make us think we can fly like a butterfly. Gravity tells us very vividly that such choices are wrong. These are examples of learning from "natural law."

True followers of Jesus believe that all of the above moral law and natural law applies to us today too. However, there are many instructions in the Bible that had only temporary application. Obviously, when God commanded Jonah to go preach repentance in Nineveh, this does not mean we should all go to Nineveh. Similarly when God commanded Israel to construct a tabernacle, offer lambs on the altar there, and so on, He was foreshadowing the coming of Christ as the perfect Lamb of God to take away the sin of the world. The Book of Hebrews shows how Israel's whole ceremonial law was fulfilled in Christ. Perhaps a little less obviously, when God commanded Israel's civil law about kosher foods, punishments for various crimes, how to farm and make clothes, and so on, He was giving laws for the nation Israel, given the messed-up world around them at that time, not for followers of Jesus in our time. Today many who criticize the Bible get these various types of God's commands all mixed up as they try to make sick jokes about the Bible. That's part of our messed-up world in our time.

6 MOTIVES MATTER

Hi, Brook and Ryan,

In Chapter 5 we saw that for kids who want to grow up in Christ the goal of the Christian life is to glorify God and that the patterns of the Christian life are primarily Scripture and Christ, secondarily natural law. Now we'll look at the aspect of motives.

The motives of the Christian life are primarily love; secondarily pleasure, gratitude, fear, duty, and so on.

It seems most people know that Christians are to be loving people. They are right about that. A scholar asked Jesus,

> "Teacher, which is the most important commandment in the law of Moses?" Jesus replied, "'You must love the LORD your God with all your heart, all your soul, and all your mind.' This is the first and greatest commandment. A second is equally important: 'Love your neighbor as yourself.' The entire law and all the demands of the prophets are based on these two commandments." (Matthew 22:36–40)

Committed followers of Jesus primarily love God so much that they gladly are motivated to reflect God's character of infinite love, truth, and holiness as He describes in His moral law in the Bible. All rebellion against God's perfect will for us expresses a lack in our love for Him.

Motives are clearly important. A wrong motive for doing right can make that action wrong; a good motive (like love) does not make a wrong action right. For example, telling a lie or stealing for loving motives, does not make that lying or stealing right.

Most people in our time don't know about the different types of love, expressed by different words for love in the Greek language in which the New Testament (NT) was written. In fact, most people likely have hardly a clue what they actually mean when they say "love." For example, if they say "I love chocolate ice cream" do they mean the same as if they say "I love you"? If they mean something different, then how is one "love" different from another? If they say "I love you," do they mean they feel enthralled affection? The Greek language uses different words to mean different kinds of "love" relationships. Notice differences among the following four Greek words where English simply says "love."

- *Phileo* – a strong friendship-love with mutual positive feelings; companionship (21 times in the New Testament)
- *Agape* – an altruistic, voluntary, unconditional, self-sacrificing love that always decides for the other's well-being, regardless of feelings or circumstances (106 times in the NT)
- *Storge* – a natural family affection or patriotic love for one's country, for example, the natural love between relatives (in the NT only where it is combined with another word, for example, Romans 12:10)
- *Eros* – a passionate romantic sexual love between husband and wife, largely emotional affection and physical attraction; also a self-centred desire or lust to possess for oneself, a gripping affection ("in love"), a passion that tends to fade; for example, we *eros*-love some foods, material things, a sweetheart, or sex partner (not used in the NT).

Most romantic poetry, music, literature, TV, and movies focus on a feeling-based romantic sexual love, which the Greeks would describe as *eros*, after the Greek mythical god of love. But the word *eros* is not used in the New Testament. *Agape* is used in all the great New Testament "love" passages, for example, 1 Corinthians 13 and 1 John 4:7–11 (quoted earlier). *Agape* is an altruistic decision-based love that always wills to be patient and kind, and never jealous, boastful, proud, rude, or irritable. It keeps no record of being wronged; it never demands its own way; it does not rejoice about injustice but rejoices whenever the truth wins out. It is always hopeful, and endures through every circumstance (1 Corinthians 13:4–7). It is focused on choosing right attitudes and actions, not on feelings.

God so *agape*-loved the world that He sent Christ to save us from our sin (John 3:16). Jesus said people should recognize us by our *agape*-love for others (John 13:35). Paul urges us to love each other with genuine affection, and take delight in honoring each other (Romans 12:10). Here Paul combines *philia* and *storge* into one word: *philostorgos*, which NLT translates as "genuine affection." Jesus said we should *agape*-love even our enemies (Matthew 5:44), something not taught in any other world religion. This means we should *agape*-love even people we many not *phileo*-like as friends.

Some of God's expectations are not easy or fun, so we need to learn *agape*-love. We all need true friends with whom to share our deepest thoughts and feelings in *phileo*-love. We also need to learn a deep family affection, or *storge*-love, among fellow Christians in our spiritual family, whether or not we *phileo*-like them all as friends.

Remember how Peter denied Christ three times on the night before Christ was crucified, and then after Christ rose He asked Peter three times whether Peter "loved" Him (John 21:15–17)? The really interesting part of this story is that Christ first asked Peter twice if he *agape*-loved Him, but Peter twice replied that he *phileo*-loved Him. The third time Christ asked Peter whether he actually *phileo*-loved Him (as a friend). That troubled Peter, and he confirmed that he indeed *phileo*-loved Him. The obvious question for us is, how do we love Christ? Is it merely as a friend in *phileo*-love, or is it in self-sacrificing *agape*-love?

Although the word *eros* is not used in the New Testament, the concept of *eros*-love appears there several times, always as the special love between husband and wife, which is supremely shown in the "one-flesh" sexual union of sexual intercourse. In Matthew 19:3–9 (NIV) when Jesus was asked about His views on divorce, He pointed back to the Adam and Eve creation story:[36]

> Some Pharisees came to him to test him. They asked, "Is it lawful for a man to divorce his wife for any and every reason?"
> "Haven't you read," he replied, "that at the beginning the Creator 'made them male and female,' and said, 'For this reason a man will leave his father and mother and be united to his wife, and the two will become one flesh'? [6] So they are no longer two, but one flesh. Therefore what God has joined together, let no one separate."
> "Why then," they asked, "did Moses command that a man give his wife a certificate of divorce and send her away?"
> Jesus replied, "Moses permitted you to divorce your wives because your hearts were hard. But it was not this way from the beginning. I tell you that anyone who divorces his wife, except for sexual immorality, and marries another woman commits adultery."

Although the word *eros* does not appear in this story, when Jesus quotes Genesis 1:27 that the husband and wife "will become one flesh," most likely both Jesus and Moses in Genesis are really talking about the concept of *eros*-love that God most beautifully designed in the experience of sexual intercourse for only a husband and wife to enjoy. This ultimate expression of intimate love between husband and wife is likely the highest human experience of spiritual, emotional, and physical ecstasy available to us humans and as such may come as close as humanly possible to the infinite love that God the Father, Son, and Holy Spirit have enjoyed in the one being of God for all eternity. This too is likely part of what God means in Genesis 1:26–28 (NIV) in the story of God's creating Adam and Eve:

> Then God said, "Let us make mankind in our image, in our likeness, so that they may rule over the fish in the sea and the birds in the sky, over the livestock and all the wild animals, and over all the creatures that move along the ground." So God created mankind in his own image, in the image of God he created them; male and female he created them. God blessed them and said to them, "Be fruitful and increase in number; fill the earth and subdue it."

When God commanded Adam and Eve to "Be fruitful and increase in number; fill the earth," He also had designed their bodies and minds to want to do just that. That's called "sex," or "sexual intercourse," or "making love." This may be the only one of God's commands that people have ever obeyed so completely. In Christ, moms and dads know just how holy, beautiful, loving, and wonderful this dimension of married love can be. Most Christian moms and dads also regard the "sex act" as so sacred, precious, and private that they really prefer not to discuss it with anyone, except maybe a doctor or a Christian counsellor if they are having some difficulties related to it. Most are embarrassed to discuss this with their own kids. That's because it is just too intimate and private. That's why Hebrews 13:4 (The Message) speaks of the sacredness of sexual intimacy between wife and husband. Genesis 2:25 says, Now the man and his wife were both naked, but they felt no shame. Genesis 1:31 reports, Then God looked over all he had made, and he saw that it was very good! Does this sound a bit strange to you that a naked man and woman are seen by God as "very good"? It won't once you are married.

In Genesis 4:1 we read, Now Adam had sexual relations with his wife, Eve, and she became pregnant. In Matthew 1:25 we read Joseph did not have sexual relations with his bride, Mary, till after Jesus was born. Biblically, God invented *eros*-love, but only for marriage.

In the middle of the Bible is the very romantic Song of Songs. According to British pastor David Pawson, this love song is an analogy between King Solomon's passionate romance with a poor shepherd girl who lived near the king's country estate and God's passionate love relationship with His bride – His covenant people, Israel, in the Old Testament and the Christian church in the New Testament. The Bible ends with the marriage banquet of the Lamb (Christ).[37] Paul writes in Ephesians 5:22–33 that true Christians are the bride of Christ, the most intimate loving relationship, a fantastic honour and a very public role.

Brook and Ryan, this is what you want to look forward to when you get married. Some have suggested that the purposes of marriage include procreation (conceiving and raising babies), pleasure (the thrills of sexual intercourse, family life, and so on), purity (having sex with no others), partnership (lifelong friendship of wife and husband), protection (from loneliness, from foolish choices we sometimes make alone, from disease, and so on), and pattern (how wife and husband reflect the love relationship between the church and Christ).

Of course many in-Christ adults never marry but find great fulfillment as singles, as did Paul, Christ, and millions of others. That may also be God's call for you, Brook and Ryan.

And so we see, Brook and Ryan, that in the Bible our primary motive for following the pattern our Lord lays out for becoming whole as we grow up and follow Jesus must be our love for Him. This puts our love and obedience to God's law in proper perspective and in perfect harmony. For example, David wrote in Psalm 119:159–160, See how I love your commandments, LORD. Give back my life because of your unfailing love. The very essence of your words is truth. Those in our time who argue that there is a contradiction between love and obedience to God's law misunderstand both. God's moral law is one expression of His love for us. Our obedience to God's moral law is one expression of our love for Him.

Jesus taught His followers: "If you love me, obey my commandments. And I will ask the Father, and he will give you another Advocate, who will never leave you.... Those who accept my commandments and obey them are the ones who love me. And because they love me, my Father will love them. And I will love them and reveal myself to each of them." (John 14:15–16, 21)

A few verses later, in John 15:9–11, Jesus adds, "I have loved you even as the Father has loved me. Remain in my love. When you obey my commandments, you remain in my love, just as I obey my Father's commandments and remain in his love. I have told you these things so that you will be filled with my joy. Yes, your joy will overflow!"

John adds in 1 John 5:1–3, Everyone who believes that Jesus is the Christ has become a child of God. And everyone who loves the Father loves his children, too. *We know we love God's children if we love God and obey his commandments. Loving God means keeping his commandments, and his commandments are not burdensome.* (Emphasis added.)

From Brook,

Some kids say they don't live by rules. Rules are just no fun.

From Ms. Barb,

Years ago, six little puppies were born in my kitchen. In the beginning, they lived inside a box, within walls or boundaries. They felt safe in their box. One day, I placed them on a blanket in my living room, with no walls or boundaries. They were terrified. God's rules, or boundaries, are like that. They provide safety and at the same time, we feel a sense of freedom within them. People who do not belong to Christ see these rules as restrictive. People who call themselves Christian but choose to live no differently than non-Christians ignore the boundaries Jesus set up for our protection. When we love Jesus, we choose to please Him. The Bible calls Him our Bridegroom. As His bride, I want to do what He says, wouldn't you?

Kids who think God's commands are hard are not in love with Christ, the Bridegroom of Christians. Growing up in Christ requires much skill in building positive relationships with other people, both those who agree with your values and those who don't. Likely the easiest positive relationships to build are with others in your family, a *storge*-love with your parents, brothers and sisters and other relatives. Next you want to pick your friends wisely (especially those who agree with your values) in a *phileo*-love, a strong friendship-love where you each deeply appreciate the others, even if you sometimes disagree and get upset with each other. In your younger years these friends are likely to be of the same sex as you. As you grow into your teens, your circle of friends is likely to include others of the opposite sex, according to God's good design for you. There may come a time in your later teens or twenties that you will feel a special *eros*-love attraction for one person of the opposite sex. Hopefully, you are already praying for God's wisdom and good direction for you at that stage of growing up in Christ, knowing that your brain will not be fully developed till you are about 25. Hopefully, you are already making some notes of the qualities you really want in a potential marriage partner and qualities you really don't want in a potential marriage partner. This means that you'll not want to date anyone who does not fit into your preferred qualities category, in case you "fall in love" (*eros*-love attraction) with such a person. Whole kids are wise enough to know that *eros*-love attractions tend to fade, so that successful marriages are built on a husband and wife who really *agape*-love each other, whether or not at any certain time of their lives they feel *eros*-love attractions or even p*hileo*-love friendships.

In-Christ kids are wise enough to know that some kids will believe and behave in ways they really don't like. Hence, we can't really be "best friends" with everyone. But we can still *agape*-love and respect everyone as created by God in His image – even bullies. In-Christ kids never bully anyone, but they try to be brave enough to stand up to bullies and urge them to learn to treat everyone with *agape*-love and respect, whether or not they claim to follow Jesus as Lord of their lives.

AT OUR HOUSE

1. **Discuss with your parents how the four loves show in your daily lives.**
2. **Discuss with your parents how the four loves should affect your choice of friends and future dates.**

Bonus: Ask your Sunday school teacher or club leader how the four loves should affect your choice of friends and future dates.

So the primary motive for our glorifying God and following His perfect will for us is our love for Him in response to His love for us. But God recognizes that we are fallen, messed-up sinners, even as Christians. For this reason He also encourages us to obey His moral law by secondary motives such as pleasure, gratitude, fear, and duty. Many messed-up people in our time think of the Bible as a book of rules designed to destroy all our fun. They are quite wrong about that. God designed our minds and bodies to enjoy many kinds of pleasure for His greater glory and our fun. Think about Psalm 16:11, You will show me the way of life, granting me the *joy* of your presence and the *pleasures* of living with you forever. (Emphasis added.) God invented fun (including all wholesome pleasures), just like He invented love.

Among the wholesome pleasures God invented are the unnumbered joys of this life (for example, laughing with family and friends, enjoying the breath-taking beauties of the night skies, sunsets, mountains, lakes, trees, flowers of meadows, gardens and homes, the thrills and loves of marriage, sex, and families, friends, music, art, sports, games, travel, learning, work, church, salvation, worship, and so on).

Who can begin to imagine all the pleasures that God has prepared for us after we leave this earth? Our rewards are literally "out of this world!" Daniel 12:3 reads: Those who are wise will shine as bright as the sky, and those who lead many to righteousness will shine like the stars forever. In Matthew 25:23 Jesus says, "The master said, 'Well done, my good and faithful servant. You have been faithful in handling this small amount, so now I will give you many more responsibilities. Let's celebrate together!'" Paul writes in 1 Corinthians 9:25 Everyone who competes in the games goes into strict training. They do it to get a crown that will not last, but we do it to get a crown that will last forever (NIV). In 2 Timothy 4:8 Paul writes, And now the prize awaits me – the crown of righteousness, which the Lord, the righteous Judge, will give me on the day of his return. And the prize is not just for me but for all who eagerly look forward to his appearing. James writes, God blesses those who patiently endure testing and temptation. Afterward they will receive the crown of life that God has promised to those who love him (James 1:12). Peter tells us, And when the Great Shepherd appears, you will receive a crown of never-ending glory and honor (1 Peter 5:4).

Who can begin to imagine all the pleasures that God has prepared for us in heaven? John gives us a glimpse of the worship there in Revelation 4:1–3, 9–11:

> Then as I looked, I saw a door standing open in heaven, and the same voice I had heard before spoke to me like a trumpet blast. The voice said, 'Come up here, and I will show you what must

> happen after this.' And instantly I was in the Spirit and I saw a throne in heaven and someone sitting on it. The one sitting on the throne was as brilliant as gemstones – like jasper and carnelian. And the glow of an emerald circled his throne like a rainbow....
>
> "Whenever the living beings give glory and honor and thanks to the one sitting on the throne (the one who lives forever and ever), the twenty-four elders fall down and *worship* the one sitting on the throne (the one who lives forever and ever). And they lay their crowns before the throne and say, *'You are worthy, O Lord our God, to receive glory and honor and power. For you created all things, and they exist because you created what you pleased'.*(Emphasis added.)

Too bad that so many people don't realize that our God invented pleasure, joy, and fun. Our God has never been the kill-joy grump that so many people imagine Him to be.

Gratitude is another powerful positive motive for growing up whole and doing what's right. In 2 Corinthians 5: 11, 14–15 Paul writes,

> Because we understand our fearful responsibility to the Lord, we work hard to persuade others.... *Christ's love controls us.* Since we believe that Christ died for all, we also believe that we have all died to our old life. He died for everyone so that those who receive his new life will *no longer live for themselves.* Instead, they will *live for Christ,* who died and was raised for them. (Emphasis added.)

In Romans 5:5–11 Paul adds,

> For we know how dearly God loves us, because he has given us the Holy Spirit to fill our hearts with his love.
>
> When we were utterly helpless, Christ came at just the right time and died for us sinners. Now, most people would not be willing to die for an upright person, though someone might perhaps be willing to die for a person who is especially good. But God showed his great love for us by sending Christ to die for us while

AT OUR HOUSE

1. **Brainstorm what wholesome fun you especially enjoy and why.**
2. **With your parents brainstorm what unwholesome "fun" some messed-up people enjoy and why they are not smart.**

Bonus: Invite some Christian friends outside your immediate family to share a time of wholesome fun with you.

> we were still sinners. And since we have been made right in God's sight by the blood of Christ, he will certainly save us from God's condemnation. For since our friendship with God was restored by the death of his Son while we were still his enemies, we will certainly be saved through the life of his Son. So *now we can rejoice* in our wonderful new relationship with God because our Lord Jesus Christ has made us friends of God. (Emphasis added.)

An old chorus celebrates this with these words:

> After all He's done for me; After all He's done for me;
> How can I do less than give Him my best and live for Him completely; After all He's done for me!

Some people avoid breaking speed limits or parking laws simply out of fear of getting a ticket. The same applies to other misbehaviours.

Since before Adam and Eve fell into sin, there has been a war between good and evil in our world (the theme of unnumbered novels, movies, and so on.). The serpent who tempted Eve to disobey God was clearly on the side of evil. God, being a God of *agape*-love, has always given Satan, his fallen angles, and people who choose to follow them, the freedom to rebel against God, Who is always on the side of good, right, and truth. As an expression of God's *agape*-love He has provided an eternal home where Satan, his fallen angles, and people who chose to follow them can continue their rebellion against God as much as they like. That eternal home Jesus called hell

AT OUR HOUSE

1. **With your parents, try to imagine what your believing relatives who have gone to heaven might be doing now.**
2. **Ask your parents how you might reply to one of your friends who says, "That pie in the sky when you die is a bunch of fairy tales."**

Bonus: Ask your Sunday school teacher or club leader what they imagine might be the best part of enjoying heaven.

(Matthew 5:22, 29, 30; 7:13; 10:28; 16:18; 18:9; 23:15, 33). Paul mentioned it (Romans 8:38), as did James (3:6) and Peter (2 Peter 2:4). John called it the "fiery lake of burning sulfur" (Revelation 19:20) and a "lake of fire" (Revelation 20:14–15). All indications are that it is indeed an eternity to be feared. And yet many messed-up people today say they would much rather go there for eternity than to spend eternity where everyone is worshipping the God Whom they hate more than anything. Others believe that our death on earth simply ends our story so there is no hell to be feared. Of course, believing such ideas does not make them true.

Sometimes we may not be motivated to do what's right out of love for Jesus, a desire for the pleasures God offers us, or the fear of the bad consequences of our rebellion against God's wise preferences for us. In that case God spells out our duties to think and do what's good and right. Most of the pattern of life we've already considered could fit here (such as, the Ten Commandments, Jesus' Sermon on the Mount, and other moral law teachings). In Ephesians 6:1; 3–19 Paul simply declares,

> Children, obey your parents because you belong to the Lord, for this is *the right thing to do....*
>
> Fathers, do not provoke your children to anger by the way you treat them. Rather, bring them up with the discipline and instruction that comes from the Lord.
>
> Slaves, obey your earthly masters with deep respect and fear. Serve them sincerely as you would serve Christ. Try to please them all the time, not just when they are watching you. As slaves of Christ, *do the will of God with all your heart.* Work with enthusiasm, as though you were working for the Lord rather than for people. Remember that the Lord will reward each one of us for the good we do, whether we are slaves or free.
>
> Masters, treat your slaves in the same way. Don't threaten them; remember, you both have the same Master in heaven, and he has no favorites.
>
> A final word: Be strong in the Lord and in his mighty power. Put on all of God's armor so that you will be able to stand firm against all strategies of the devil. For we are not fighting against flesh-and-blood enemies, but against evil rulers and authorities of the unseen world, against mighty powers in this dark world, and against evil spirits in the heavenly places.

> Therefore, put on every piece of God's armor so you will be *able to resist the enemy* in the time of evil. Then after the battle you will still be standing firm. *Stand your ground,* putting on the belt of truth and the body armor of God's righteousness. For shoes, put on the peace that comes from the Good News so that you will be fully prepared. In addition to all of these, hold up the shield of faith to stop the fiery arrows of the devil. Put on salvation as your helmet, and take the sword of the Spirit, which is the word of God.
>
> Pray in the Spirit at all times and on every occasion. *Stay alert and be persistent in your prayers* for all believers everywhere.
>
> And pray for me, too. (Emphasis added.)

The Bible teaches us many other duties, including paying taxes and obeying government (except when governments order us to violate God's moral law).

But pursuing a biblical goal by a biblical pattern and with biblical motives seems humanly impossible. And it is impossible, without supernatural power. You really need the next chapter.

7 IN CHRIST WE HAVE POWER

Hi, Brook and Ryan,

In Chapter 5 we saw that for kids who want to grow up in Christ, the goal of the Christian life is to glorify God and that the patterns of the Christian life are primarily Scripture and Christ, secondarily natural law.

In Chapter 6 we saw that for kids who want to grow up in Christ, the motives of the Christian life are primarily love; secondarily pleasure, gratitude, fear, duty, and so on.

Here we'll see that kids who grow up in Christ have supernatural power.

The Power of the Christian life: The Holy Spirit

That supernatural power is the Holy Spirit, who Jesus promised just before He ascended to heaven. He told His followers in Acts 1:5, 8,

> "John baptized with water, but in just a few days you will be baptized with the Holy Spirit....
> But you will receive power when the Holy Spirit comes upon you. And you will be my witnesses, telling people about me everywhere – in Jerusalem, throughout Judea, in Samaria, and to the ends of the earth."

Amazingly, Jesus told His followers, "But when you are arrested and stand trial, don't worry in advance about what to say. Just say what God tells you at that time, for it is not you who will be speaking, but the Holy Spirit" (Mark

13:11). In Luke 12:11–12 Jesus told His followers, "And when you are brought to trial in the synagogues and before rulers and authorities, don't worry about how to defend yourself or what to say, for the Holy Spirit will teach you at that time what needs to be said." Isn't that awesomely empowering?

Even Jesus depended on the Holy Spirit's power to overcome temptations to sin, just like we do. Then Jesus returned to Galilee, filled with the Holy Spirit's power (Luke 4:14).

Concerning prayer, Luke reported what Jesus said:

> At that same time Jesus was filled with the joy of the Holy Spirit, and he said, 'O Father, Lord of heaven and earth, thank you for hiding these things from those who think themselves wise and clever, and for revealing them to the childlike. Yes, Father, it pleased you to do it this way' (Luke 10:21).

Do you ever feel this when some messed-up people mock you for believing God answers your prayers or for believing in the Holy Spirit?

From Ryan:

How about if sometimes I really don't feel that the Holy Spirit is helping me in tight spots?

From Uncle Al:

Sometimes I ask kids, "Do you have four fingers and a thumb on your right hand? Can you pray, 'Lord Jesus, help me now!' as you close your four fingers and thumb?" Jesus said the Holy Spirit will give you supernatural power to do right when that is what you need – whether or not you actually feel it at the time. After Moses died, God encouraged Joshua before he entered Canaan in Joshua 1:6–9:

> *"Be strong and courageous,* for you are the one who will lead these people to possess all the land I swore to their ancestors I would give them. *Be strong and very courageous. Be careful to obey* all the instructions Moses gave you. Do not deviate from them, turning either to the right or to the left. Then you will be successful in everything you do. *Study this Book of Instruction continually. Meditate on it day and night so* you will be sure to *obey everything* written in it. Only then will you prosper and succeed in all you do. This is my command – *be strong and courageous! Do not be afraid*

> *or discouraged.* For the *LORD your God is with you*_wherever you go." (Emphasis added.)

In John 14:15–20 he tells how Jesus encouraged His followers:

> *"If you love me, obey my commandments.* And I will ask the Father, and he will give you another Advocate, who will never leave you. He is the *Holy Spirit, who leads into all truth.* The world cannot receive him, because it isn't looking for him and doesn't recognize him. But you know him, because he lives with you now and later will be in you. No, I will not abandon you as orphans – I will come to you. Soon the world will no longer see me, but you will see me. Since I live, you also will live. When I am raised to life again, you will *know that I am in my Father, and you are in me, and I am in you."* (Emphasis added.)

From Brook:

Exactly how does the Holy Spirit "lead" us "into all truth"? Sometimes I really don't feel that He is answering my prayers.

From Ms. Barb:

Most times the Holy Spirit leads us into all truth by helping us understand what the Bible means as we read it, and how it applies to our situation. Sometimes He might seem like a still small voice whispering in your mind, "This way is right" or "That way is wrong." God answers our prayers in three different ways. He says "yes" or "no" but He also says "wait." This can feel as if He isn't answering at all sometimes. Sometimes we're really just not sure. Then it may be best to discuss the issue with your parents or with a strong Christian friend who will pray with you to choose the wise way to grow up in Christ. It may help you to pray for special Holy Spirit guidance as you think how He wants you to decide what's right or wrong on issues where sincere Bible-believing Christians disagree. In Book Five, *Deciding What's Right or Wrong*, this topic is discussed in detail for teens, ages 13 to 19.

8 SHOULD WE NEVER SAY "THAT'S WRONG"?

(Caution: some issues in Chapters 8 to11 may not be suitable for every 8- to 12-year-old tween.)

Ever since Adam and Eve fell into sin, all humans have been sinners and all nature has been cursed by sin, so that we all live in a very messed-up world. Part of that mess is the some 1,200 religions that various people now follow. Even in the Christian community we now have some 35,000 denominations. Obviously these are not all right on every question of belief and behaviour. Hence, it's not surprising that a growing number of people around the world dismiss all religions as false. Many believe that atheist mocking of all religions is the only smart thing to do. All kids growing up will likely meet such people and should not be surprised when they do. Part of growing up in Christ is learning to *agape*-love and respect all people, including those who think Bible-believing Christians are simply stupid or hateful for disagreeing with them about any belief or behaviour. Healthy kids learn that they can still be friends with other kids who disagree with them about anything, so long as they disagree respectfully and their disagreement does not turn into bullying on either side.

Bullying can be an example of a disagreement that gets out of control. Ever since Cain got mad at Abel and killed him, most people at some time have bullied others, even if they did not kill them. Some have angrily hit their opponents; some have called them insulting names; some have shut others out of their fun times. In our time, some use email or social media to say nasty things to people they don't like, or spread gossip about them to make them feel bad or to ruin their reputations with school classmates, and so on. We have already talked about some strategies that may help to deal with bullying. The first step always is to make sure you never bully anyone, no matter what they believe, say, do, or are. Often this is not easy. We all need the Holy Spirit's supernatural power to overcome our own temptations to bully others.

Some people are of different races, cultures, languages, or religions from yours. Some people are smarter or not as smart as you. Some people are taller, shorter, fatter, or thinner than you. Each of us is uniquely created in God's own image. Some boys bully girls simply because they are girls. Some girls bully boys simply because they are boys. Racism is wrong. Sexism is wrong. There is no sound reason for us to bully others or for others to bully us. All bullying betrays a lack of love and respect for others as God commanded us to show to everyone. God loves everyone in the world (John 3:16) and so should we (Matthew 22:37–40).

Sometimes groups of friends, sports teams, gangs, companies, nations, and other organizations bully others. Kids who are growing up in Christ bravely do what they can to stop such misbehaviour, even if their efforts are unsuccessful sometimes. They seek help from parents, teachers, pastors, sometimes police, or anyone who might help stop the bullying.

In the war between good and evil, most people see themselves as being on the side of good and right. Naturally, this means that most people believe those who disagree with them must be on the side of evil and wrong. We all evaluate beliefs and behaviours; we embrace some as good and right and reject others as evil and wrong.

From Ryan,

But didn't Jesus say we should never judge anyone?

From Uncle Al:

Likely most people think Jesus' statement in Matthew 7:1 (NIV) "Do not judge, or you too will be judged" means we should never judge anyone. But notice how Jesus explains (Matthew 7:1–6, NIV):

> "For in the same way you judge others, you will be judged, and with the measure you use, it will be measured to you. *Why do you look at the speck of sawdust in your brother's eye and pay no attention to the plank in your own eye?* How can you say to your brother, 'Let me take the speck out of your eye,' when all the time there is a plank in your own eye? *You hypocrite, first take the plank out of your own eye, and then you will see clearly to remove the speck from your brother's eye."*

Does this mean that it is wrong to say bullying is wrong? Would saying that be a case of judging the bully? Yes, it would, especially if we tell the bully to stop the bullying behaviour by showing hate for the bully or passing "final judgment" on him, such as only God can do. Is it wrong to say racism is wrong? Is it wrong to say sexism is wrong? Most people who say, "Do not judge," are quite quick to judge racism and sexism as wrong.

In Ephesians 5:11 we read: "Take no part in the worthless deeds of evil and darkness; instead, expose them." The most loving response to bullies is to get them to stop their bullying behaviour and to embrace Christ's love for them. The same applies to all messed-up people who embrace messed-up beliefs and behaviours.

Some people today feel they are entitled to never be offended by anyone for anything they say or do. Some kids today feel they are entitled to always be praised, rewarded, or affirmed for anything they say or do. But think about this. Would this not mean that no one should ever disagree with anyone about anything? But that is logically impossible. Would this not mean that no one should ever fail at anything? But the real world does not work that way. Kids who grow up believing they are entitled to success always, are in for some rude awakenings. Kids who wish to grow up in Christ need to understand that in the adult world people fail sometimes, people are wrong sometimes, and the most loving thing anyone can do for us when we are wrong is to tell us so and show us how to correct our mistakes. That's not bullying. But for anyone to demand an entitlement to unending success is another form of bullying and it is wrong.

From Brook,

So what's the right way to tell the bully to stop the bullying?

From Ms. Barb,

Bullies look for someone who doesn't love themselves. The best way to stop a bully is to do what God asks of us. Love who you are in Christ, who God made you to be. Then a bully has no place to ridicule or demean you, even if they try to do so.

In Matthew 7 Jesus tells us to check our own attitudes and behaviours before we correct others. Remember that we all mess up sometimes, so we all need to be corrected sometimes. Also, remember that we are all created in God's image[38] so we need to *agape*-love and respect everyone, even those who misbehave. This does not suggest we need to agree their beliefs are true or their behaviours are good and right.

Lawyer and peacemaker Ken Sande has been helping people resolve their differences since the early 1980s. He recommends "charitable judgment" of others who advocate false beliefs and who practice bad behaviours.[39] He understands Matthew 7:1 this way:

> What [Jesus] is warning us about is our inclination to make critical judgments in the negative sense, which involves looking for others' faults and, without valid and sufficient reason, forming unfavorable opinions of their qualities, words, actions, or motives. In simple terms, it means looking for the worst in others.

Whole kids don't do that. Instead, they make "charitable judgments," which Sande defines as meaning

> that out of love for God, you strive to believe the best about others until you have facts to prove otherwise. In

> other words, if you can reasonably interpret facts in two possible ways, God calls you to embrace the positive interpretation over the negative, or at least to postpone making any judgment at all until you can acquire conclusive facts.[40]

Only God knows everything. Only God is infinitely loving, truthful and holy. Hence, only God is the final Judge on all beliefs and behaviours; we are not.

But Jesus urges us a few verses later (Matthew 7:15–20) to

> "Beware of false prophets who come disguised as harmless sheep but are really vicious wolves. You can identify them by their fruit, that is, by the way they act. Can you pick grapes from thorn bushes, or figs from thistles? A good tree produces good fruit, and a bad tree produces bad fruit. A good tree can't produce bad fruit, and a bad tree can't produce good fruit. So every tree that does not produce good fruit is chopped down and thrown into the fire. Yes, just as you can identify a tree by its fruit, so you can identify people by their actions."

In other words, Jesus wants us to identify those "false prophets" whose beliefs and

AT OUR HOUSE

1. **Discuss what most people mean when they say "judge not." Do any people actually live like that?**
2. **Discuss your parents' views about those who feel entitled to never be offended.**
3. **Discuss Ken Sande's ideas about "charitable judgements."**

Bonus: For one week, try to keep a record of how many "charitable judgments" you hear from others and how many "uncharitable judgments" you hear. The next week try to keep a record of how many "charitable judgments" you say to others and how many "uncharitable judgments" you say to others. Then review these lists with a Christian adult you respect.

behaviours are wrong, but do so with charitable judgments. They come to us "disguised as harmless sheep but are really vicious wolves," warns Jesus. Some of those "false prophets" may be very highly educated "experts" in the eyes of the unbelieving world. Learning to practise such charitable judgments is an important part of growing up in Christ. Their impressive "research" does not mean that their conclusions are always right and true. It takes a lot of critical thinking and *agape*-love to detect the "vicious wolves" that are "disguised as harmless sheep." This is not a "soft love"[41] that never says any belief or behaviour is wrong. "Soft love" is really self-love, mostly concerned never to offend anyone and so keep peace at any price. Such "soft love" leaves the people who try to practise it at the mercy of every messed-up belief or behaviour they encounter in this messed-up world. Clearly, Jesus and his disciples were not like that at all, nor should we be.

In all human history some people have argued that bad is good and wrong is right. This happens in our time too. Paul says of such people (Romans 1:21–22, 32), As a result, their minds became dark and confused. Claiming to be wise, they instead became utter fools.... They know God's justice requires that those who do these things deserve to die, yet they do them anyway. Worse yet, they encourage others to do them, too. Kids who want to grow up in Christ need clear understandings of what is actually bad or good and wrong or right. Sometimes the most loving thing we can do for others is to tell them the truth, even if sometimes the truth hurts. This is called "tough love." *Agape*-love requires that we be graceful when we tell others the truth, especially if the truth is painful. John describes Jesus as coming to earth to reveal the Father, but to do so full of grace and truth (John 1:14 NIV).

We have already noticed several times how beautifully God has created our universe, including Adam and Eve in His image, including you, Ryan and Brook, and every human. We have noticed several times how beautifully God has created our bodies and minds for many purposes including romantic *eros*-love so that we can richly enjoy total interpersonal intimacy, including total sexual intimacy as husband and wife in a "one-flesh" union in marriage. God has beautifully designed our bodies and minds to seek such union. Puberty is the normal time that our bodies and minds begin to seek such union, even though adolescents first entering puberty are not yet mature enough physically, mentally, emotionally or spiritually to parent babies. At puberty your brain and the rest of your body are flooded with hormones that focus on sexy feelings. In fact, your brain will keep on growing till you are about 25. The last part of your brain to mature is the thinking, reasoning, self-control, responsible decision-making part. That's why some kids are surprised when they conceive babies sooner than they thought possible (some as young as nine). That's why Chapter 2 mentioned that at puberty most girls and boys first experience sexual arousal. What prompts sexual arousal can vary widely among girls and boys, including things like private fantasies with no other person present, looking at an attractive member of the opposite sex (or pictures of them on TV, in movies, on the Internet, and elsewhere), simple or passionate kissing, caressing, and other touching.

Some parents fail to prepare their adolescent tweens and teens adequately for puberty and for responsible moral values concerning sex. So schools have been doing more of this recently. Unfortunately, much of what secular schools teach concerning sex contradicts both medical science and the Bible. Hence, kids who really want to grow up in Christ need better medical, scientific and biblical understandings of this very important topic than what they may learn from friends, TV, Internet or even schools and churches. For example, many secular sex education (ed) programs teach students the names of sexual body parts of males and females and how they fit together to conceive babies, but fail to emphasize how important it is for many physical, emotional, and mental health reasons to save sexual intercourse and other sexual experiences for marriage. Even if the option of abstaining from all sexual contacts between boys and girls is mentioned in passing as an option, most secular sex ed programs assume that kids will rarely abstain. Often in health classes in about grades 4 to 7 they talk about how to use condoms (usually latex rubber coverings over penises) to prevent pregnancy and avoid sexually transmitted infections (STIs). Whole kids understand that there are both benefits and dangers in such secular "comprehensive" sex ed programs, because they tend to focus on the physical dimensions of sex. Sadly, most tend to neglect the emotional, moral and spiritual dimensions, or just mention them lightly in passing. Some secular "comprehensive" sex ed programs fail to use terms like "love" and "marriage" even once. Whole kids understand their need for critical thinking in such programs.

Pre-schoolers are naturally curious about how boys and girls are different. Many tweens and teens are just as naturally curious about how sexual intercourse works. Unfortunately, because of false myths in much of what schools, friends, TV and the Internet teach them, too many tweens and teens are getting pregnant, contracting STIs (sexually transmitted infections), and breaking their hearts. Rarely will secular sources mention the risk that the first several times kids try sexual intercourse it can be quite painful, especially for the girls but also sometimes for the boys. Rarely will secular sources mention the risks that the first time kids try sexual intercourse the girl could get pregnant or that one partner could catch an STI from the other (when it is the first time for one but not for the other). Such results can have devastating effects on the rest of their lives. Whole kids need better understandings of these very important issues, ideally from their parents before the kids have to deal with these discussions in school and other sources. That is a main focus of this chapter.

Unfortunately, a major problem concerning deciding what is really right or wrong on any issue is the question, On what basis should we decide what is really right or wrong? For those who believe the Bible is God's inspired revelation, this gets easier, because we mostly need to learn from the Bible what is God's moral law, that is, what is really right or wrong. This is not always easy because there are so many interpretations of what the Bible actually teaches. Those who reject the Bible's authority think they can decide what is really right or wrong on the basis of reason or personal feelings. But there are even more interpretations of what is really right or wrong on the basis of reason. Too often these disputes boil down to which view people "like" (personal feelings) – not a very sound basis for deciding what is really right or wrong. Some people may even look to "experts" to tell them what is really right or wrong on the basis of reason. Of course, unless these experts can show us how their opinions are based on clear, unbiased facts, they may also be telling us mostly what they like (personal feelings) – that is, what subjective basis has given them confidence that they actually have sound reasons for their conclusions. Secular author George Orwell wisely said, "The further a society drifts from truth, the more it will hate those who speak it."[42]

From Ryan,

Some people say it's better to stay innocent of the evil in the world around us. Is this true?

From Uncle Al,

Yes, it's true, Ryan, that God wants us to stay as innocent as possible about the evil in the world around us. Paul writes in Romans 16:19, I want you to be wise in doing right and to stay innocent of any wrong. That does not mean that kids growing up in Christ must be ignorant about the evil in the world. God wants us not to know from experience what doing evil feels like. We can know that stealing and killing are wrong without doing these and other evil deeds. In our times, the problem is that we are all bombarded with messages that it's not wrong to do many deeds that the Bible calls evil. Kids who want to grow up in Christ need to understand what the Bible teaches about the evil in the world and why it is wrong. Knowledge is power. Knowing God's moral law, the power of the Holy Spirit, and the love of Christ empowers kids to grow up in Christ in a messed-up world.

From Brook,

Some of my friends say that everyone can decide for themselves when they are "ready" for sex. They don't have to wait till they get married. Is this true?

From Ms. Barb,

No, it's not true, Brook, regardless of who or how many people think it is. You see, the kind of questions that kids are taught to ask in "comprehensive" secular sex ed materials to decide if or when they are "ready" for sexual intercourse tend to be grossly naive. Unmarried partners cannot predict their own feelings a day or even a week after they've experienced sexual intercourse because there is no long-term commitment between them. Especially for girls, a lifelong commitment is really important. But if you look around at some of the relationships among kids your age, you'll see that they change their minds about romantic *eros*-love all the time and tend to flit from one best friend to another. God designed sex to be a wonderful adventure when a lifelong commitment (the marriage contract) is involved, but it can leave you with a ton of guilt if that commitment is not there.

The responsible reply to the question, Am I ready for sex? is to answer the question, Am I ready for parenting? Of course, sex is about much more than making babies and parenting, but it is surely not about anything less. But "comprehensive" sex ed materials don't say that. They seem to ask, Am I ready for sex? more like the question, Am I ready to take this thrill ride with this person? That's really the wrong way to approach this question. It neglects the emotional and spiritual dimensions of every unmarried boy and girl who enters into a risky "one-flesh" union as if it were merely some fun activity without long-term consequences.

Think about it. Everyone who says that unmarried kids can decide for themselves when they are "ready" for sex are telling kids they are entitled to do anything they want sexually without criticism or consequences. That's wrong. That's not how kids who want to grow up in Christ make choices that have lifelong consequences.

Whole kids know God's love shown in Christ's death for them and live for God's glory in the power of the Holy Spirit. They control their passions and delay their God-given sexual desires till they are in a lifelong covenant with their spouses as God lovingly designed

From Brook,

Some of my friends say that everyone has sex sometime in high school or college anyhow, even those who think they can wait till they get married. Is this true?

From Ms. Barb,

No, it's not true, Brook, regardless of who or how many people think it is. The idea that everyone has sex sometime before marriage anyhow makes no more sense than saying everyone will bully others anyhow, so it's not realistic to tell them to stop – we should just make bullying safer. Both are wrong.

Too many comprehensive sex ed programs say that abstaining from sex before marriage may be a nice ideal, but it's not realistic. So they recommend that kids wait till they are sure they are ready for this big step, that they trust their partner to be free of STIs, that they trust their partner to continue a stable loving relationship with them, and that they use protection to make sure they are safer from the risk of pregnancy and getting STIs. Yes, some contraceptives provide some protection against pregnancy and against some STIs, but none of them protect your emotions, heart, and soul.

The "safer sex" view sets a low standard that won't help you grow up healthy in Christ. The only really safe way to protect your body, mind, and soul is to abstain from sex before marriage and be faithful to your spouse after marriage. Sex in marriage is God's beautiful, joyous, and holy gift to you. Be smart and do this right. Display self-control. Live by your principles. Tell your raging hormones they can wait. You are not just an animal. Keep your virginity as a special gift to your sweetheart after your wedding.

In his essay "Sex in the Real World," Matt Kaufman writes,

> Human beings aren't rutting dogs, helpless in the grip of the mating urge. We've always had sexual impulses, but we haven't always let them rule us. Not so long ago, most people really did reserve sex for marriage, for reasons both moral and practical. It *can* be done – not just by rare individuals, but by whole societies. For a long time in a lot of places, it was positively *normal.*
>
> And let's be honest: People who respond that "you can't turn back the clock" really don't want to turn back the clock. When liberals seriously oppose something, they don't facilitate it and declare it "safe": They're forever declaring "war" on one thing or another (poverty, racism, sexism, homophobia). But they don't want sexual morality back. They want all the things they like about sex with none of the burdens – stuff like disease, pregnancy and (here's a scary item) lifelong commitment. And they want it all guilt-free, which is why they like to suggest that using some latex rubber makes you "responsible."
>
> Such people like to pose as "realists," but they're really avoiding reality. They're desperately trying to preserve something – the Sexual Revolution of the '60s – that has proven, in practice, to be an unmitigated disaster.[43]

Blogger Matt Walsh writes,

> Sex is not supposed to be safe. Sex isn't supposed to be physically perilous like it often is these days – thanks, mostly, to years of "safe sex" education – but it *is* supposed to be an act of great depth and consequence. Sex is meant to be open and exposed. It's meant to bring out scary and mysterious feelings of desire and devotion....
>
> Sex itself isn't safe. On the other hand, committed relationships, fortified by the vows of marriage and reaffirmed daily by both spouses, are safe – and it is only

in this context that the inherent vulnerability of sex can be made secure and comfortable.

It's funny that in the world of petty one night stands, when someone commits the crime of being a human being who develops natural pangs of emotional closeness and affection, the other person is allowed to accuse *them* of being "weird" or "moving too fast." And when the manmade barricades fail and a human life is tragically formed, both parties can, with a straight face, say that it was an "accident."

This is like planting a seed in the ground and calling it a mistake when a tree begins to sprout because you thought the soil was infertile. You may have believed this, but still the seed is doing exactly what seeds are supposed to do, and you did exactly what a person is supposed to do if they want to make a tree grow. You may be a fool, but this was no accident.

Next, you cut down the sapling and toss it in the fire, and then you continue to plant seeds. Each time, you cry that all of these ... trees keep shooting out of the ground. When someone comes and tells you to stop planting until you're ready to deal with a forest, you weep and accuse the person of being cruel and judgmental simply because they're articulating [saying] the basic rules of botany.

Of course, this metaphor fails for one reason: everyone agrees that you shouldn't kill baby trees. No such consensus [agreement] exists when it comes to baby people....

The abstinence-before-marriage plan paints an affirmative [positive] and uplifting picture. It says, "this is something so good and so important and so joyful that you should leave it be until you grow up and find one special person to share it with."...

"Safe sex" gives you shallow joys and deep fears,

abstinence gives you deep joys and avoidable fears.[44]

Even these days, unnumbered millions are waiting till marriage, even if schools, TV, movies, popular music, and most Internet sites don't talk about them. These people are not perfect, and their marriages are not perfect, but they are much closer to the way God designed them to be. Hence, they tend to experience more love, joy, peace, sex and fulfillment, than their "safe sex" friends. The American Psychological Association's *Journal of Family Psychology* reported a recent study of 2,035 married individuals and found that couples who wait until they put a ring on it enjoy significantly more benefits than those who had sex earlier: relationship stability was rated 22 per cent higher; relationship satisfaction was rated 20 per cent higher; sexual quality of the relationship was rated 15 per cent better and communication was rated 12 per cent better.[45] Which "safer sex" program reports such data?

Depending on the friends you choose, staying chaste till you marry may not be easy, but it can be simple. Just ask yourself whom you will obey – friends who urge, "Just do it!" or God (who loves you more than anyone else loves you) Who says, "Wait till you marry!" Psalm 119:9 reads, How can a young person stay pure? By obeying your word. That's simple, even if not easy sometimes.

AT OUR HOUSE

1. **Discuss what you should say if someone insists "everyone's doing it" before marriage.**
2. **Ask for your parents' ideas about "sex is beautiful and sacred."**
3. **Ask for your parents' ideas about how "realistic" it is to ask teens to abstain from sex and bullying.**

Bonus: For one day a week, try to keep a record of how often you see or hear someone else say something about sex. For another day a week, try to keep a record of how often you think about sex without seeing or hearing someone else say something about it. Then review these lists with a Christian adult you respect.

From Brook,

Can you help us sort some of the facts from myths about contraceptives?

From Ms. Barb,

Let me try, Brook. The primary goal of contraceptives is to protect the woman from the risk of getting pregnant when she is not ready to have a baby. Some married couples who decide they are not ready to get pregnant try to time their sexual intercourse events to those times of the wife's monthly cycle when she is not fertile. This is sometimes called a "natural" or "rhythm" method of contraception. In contrast to this practice, most other methods of contraception are called "artificial contraception." Some countries and some churches don't permit their people to use artificial contraceptives.

Most contraceptives sold today do a reasonably good job of avoiding pregnancy, but only if they are used properly 100 percent of the time that men and women have sexual intercourse. Most are designed for wives, a few for husbands. One problem is that too often unmarried kids and adults fail to use contraceptives properly 100 percent of the time. The US Centers for Disease Control and Prevention provides useful charts of birth control options with typical failure rates for each concerning unintended pregnancies within one year of use.[46]

The World Health Organization (WHO) issues regular reports on the use of various contraceptives in various parts of the world (grouped in 10 broad categories).[47] The British National Health Services provides brief information on 15 types of contraceptives.[48] The pros and cons of each are best discussed with your parents. In brief, no contraceptives can guarantee that the woman will not get pregnant or that no STI will be transferred from either partner to the other. Some STIs (for example, HIV) can be transferred from either partner to the other the first time they have sexual activity, if one of them has an STI, whether or not they know that.

It may be that the high rates of teen pregnancy in spite of comprehensive sex ed programs show that these programs actually promote an unbiblical view of sex. Psychiatrist Miriam Grossman, MD, observes that the priority of most comprehensive sex ed programs is not to prevent teen pregnancies or to avoid STIs. Instead, "It's to promote a specific worldview – *sex is not an appetite to be restricted* – and rally kids toward social change."[49] (Emphasis is hers.) In her review of the New York City (NYC) sex ed program, she notes that the intended lesson is "that sex, whether in middle school, high school or adulthood, in or outside a committed monogamous relationship, is 'positive' and 'healthy'."[50] She further reports that the NYC sex ed curriculum materials "increased sexual activity and experimentation." This is described as a normal part of middle adolescent development. She clearly disagrees with the belief that this is normal or healthy, even if it is common. Dr. Grossman is particularly critical of the curriculum statement when discussing condoms: "There are two ways to avoid getting pregnant or HIV: say no to sex or use protection," so as to suggest that using a condom is as safe as abstaining from all sexual activity – not true. Abstinence is completely risk-free; using a condom is not.

Across our globe the leading provider of abortions is Planned Parenthood. They also provide contraceptives and counselling on sex issues, including telling teens "Anything within the sexual world is normal so long as it's consensual."[51] For the rest of your lives, Brook and Ryan, the secular world will likely believe this. If you believe differently, you will need to know why. Clearly, kids who want to grow up healthy in Christ don't believe that it's okay to be whipped, tied up, or strangled in hopes of gaining sexual pleasure, regardless of what Planned Parenthood says.[52] When Planned Parenthood says "Only you can decide when you're ready" for every type of sexual experience, that is not wise advice for tweens or teens who are not married for life.

Some contraceptives (for example, male and female condoms) give some protection from catching some STIs from a sex partner. In "comprehensive" sex ed programs kids are routinely taught how to use condoms because they make sexual intercourse "safer." Before we consider that claim, let's briefly introduce the more common STIs ("sexually transmitted infections," also known as "sexually transmitted diseases" or STDs, though that is a narrower concept, not including STIs transferred from a mother to a child during pregnancy or in childbirth or through blood or tissue transfers).[53]

The World Health Organization provides regularly updated fact sheets on STIs. Their December 2015 sheet reports that every day over 1 million new people get STIs. They estimate that about 500 million people get sick every year from just these four STIs: chlamydia, gonorrhea, syphilis, and trichomoniasis.[54] These four can usually be cured with timely appropriate treatment. Another four are viral infections and cannot be cured, though their symptoms can be treated. A similar report in November 2013 showed the following data: hepatitis B – over 240 million people now have it; herpes – over 530 million people now have it; HIV (human immunodeficiency virus, which causes AIDS [acquired immunodeficiency syndrome]) – over 35 million people now have it, and over 36 million people have died of it since 1980[55]; and HPV (human papilloma virus) – over 290 million people now have it. These eight cause most of the STI illnesses in the world. WHO warns that most people with an STI don't know that they have one, because they have not yet shown any symptoms. STIs that may show no symptoms include bacterial vaginosis, chlamydia, gonorrhea, HIV, HPV, pelvic

AT OUR HOUSE

1. **Ask your parents what they believe about the use of "artificial contraceptives" by *married* couples today and why.**
2. **Ask your parents what they believe about the use of "artificial contraceptives" by *unmarried* couples today and why.**

inflammatory disease (PID), syphilis and trichomoniasis.[56] WHO also warns that STIs are caused by "more than 30 different bacteria, viruses and parasites and are spread predominantly by sexual contact, including vaginal, anal and oral sex."[57] It also warns that some STIs are spread by skin-to-skin sexual contact (for example, herpes, and genital warts), usually not covered by condoms.

Unfortunately, much of this information is not included in many secular "comprehensive" sex ed programs that kids are routinely taught in school. And where some of this information is included, the spin of the presentation is often misleading, especially by exaggerating the protection that condoms provide. For unmarrieds, the Kids Health website is right: "The only people who have no risk of getting an STD are people who haven't had sex or any kind of sexual contact."[58] The other way to be 100 percent sure you won't get an STI is to marry someone who has also had no sexual contact of any kind and have both of you be faithful to each other throughout life (and neither be raped).

In her critique of the NYC curriculum Dr. Grossman points out that condoms are sometimes promoted as 98 percent effective. That sounds good, till we notice that this rate has been shown concerning pregnancy prevention with adults' "perfect use" of condoms (that is, exactly right use, 100 percent of the time they had sex). But adults' "typical use" of condoms has shown condoms as 85 percent effective concerning pregnancy prevention. Dr. Grossman adds, "Taking into account their immaturity, use of alcohol before sex, and other factors, teens' typical use of condoms could be expected to prevent pregnancy at a much lower rate."[59] These kids keep the abortion industry busy, and many suffer emotionally for much of their lives. In a study of over 10,000 abortions, 54 percent of the women reported having used contraceptives before their pregnancy, male condoms being the most commonly used. Of condom users, 42 percent reported that the condom slipped or broke. Of the 21,902 NYC pregnancies in 2009 in girls 19 and under, 573 were in girls under 15 years of age. Dr. Grossman wonders how many of them trusted male condoms to prevent pregnancy. How many of them believed that when the NYC curriculum says "Every time a couple has sex unprotected, they risk getting pregnant" this implied that using male condoms would eliminate this risk? If so, they were wrong, and the NYC sex ed curriculum was misleading.

Similarly, the NYC curriculum leaves students unprotected from medical scientific facts about the infection rates and the physically and emotionally damaging effects of chlamydia, gonorrhea, syphilis, herpes, and HPV, the last two of which are especially prevalent. Yes, condoms do reduce the rates of pregnancy and STI infections. Conservative estimates rate their reductions of infections for herpes by 30 percent, for chlamydia, gonorrhea, and syphilis by 50 percent, for HPV by 0–70 percent. Over half of the almost 22,000 pregnant NYC teens in 2009 used no protection against STIs. Still, the NYC curriculum tells students, "Condoms are a good way to protect from STDs." Is that responsible sex ed? This depends on if one agrees that teens will have sexual intercourse anyhow, as most comprehensive sex ed programs assume. Kids who actually prefer to grow up healthy in Christ know better.

9 WHEN IS CONSENT INFORMED?

(Caution: some issues in Chapters 8 to 11 may not be suitable for every 8- to 12-year-old tween.)

It seems that bright people everywhere in every age can imagine "good reasons" for believing and doing what they like; that is, they convince themselves that they are not guilty of any wrong, because what they like is somehow right. Some even argue that they have a "human right" to do what they like on sex. This process is called "rationalizing."[60] For example, some fathers, uncles, older brothers, and friends of the family are sexually attracted to girls too young to marry.[61] They might even imagine they are helping these young girls prepare for marriage by arousing them sexually and having intercourse with them. Often these girls believe that such incestuous events are really their fault, and they may go into serious self-loathing depressions, either right away or sometimes many decades later. This also happens to some boys who are groomed for same-sex experiences by older boys or men. Sadly, sometimes older girls or women lure younger boys into sex acts of various kinds. When sexual intercourse happens without normal sexual arousal and informed adult consent of both parties it's called "rape," whether their attacker is a friend, family member, or a stranger. Some victims of incest or rape turn to alcohol or non-prescription drugs to deal with their shame, sense of guilt, or emotional confusion. Whole healthy kids know that crimes of incest or rape are not their fault. If they see such crimes developing, they need to respond bravely by very quickly and clearly saying, "no, no, NO!" like Joseph did in the Genesis 39 account of Potiphar's wife trying to have sex with him (Potiphar was captain of king pharaoh's palace guard). They should run away and quickly tell a parent, teacher, coach, or police officer, who can help deal with such crimes.

Some predators even tease and "sweet talk" their victims into asking for sexual intercourse, so that the victims believe they were giving "informed consent" for sexual intercourse (that is, giving permission while understanding what that means). However, most governments have laws against this, for example, that no child under 16 years old is legally mature enough to give "informed consent" for sexual intercourse. Most governments also have laws against anyone getting a driver's licence before 16 or 18 years of age. Most governments also do not allow anyone to vote before age 18 or 21. And yet some sex ed "experts" teach 12-year-old kids how they should decide if they are ready to "give informed consent" for sexual intercourse. Kids who prefer to grow up in Christ see how foolish such ideas and behaviours are.

Notice that some people imagine that rape and sex without informed consent only happen with strangers – not true. A British study showed that kids are three times as likely to be lured into sex by friends or family members they know and trust as by a stranger.[62]

Informed consent is important for all cases of one person's touching another person, whether or not sexual intercourse might be in mind for either of them. Learn the difference between unsafe touch (unwanted touch) and safe touch (welcomed touch).

From Ryan,

Some of my friends say it's fun to rub their own private parts. Does the Bible say anything about this?

From Uncle Al,

Yes, it does, but maybe not as directly as we might prefer. God has beautifully designed male penises and female vaginas to fit together nicely and to sense great pleasure, even ecstasy, in normal husband and wife one-flesh sexual intercourse. No other sexual experience can actually duplicate that kind of one-flesh unifying mutual joy. Some of that physical pleasure can be aroused by hand rubbing of a male penis and a female vagina (especially the clitoris). This is called "masturbation." Jesus said that lustful looking amounts to adultery (Matthew 5:28). Most times that adolescent boys and girls masturbate they imagine having sex with someone, either real or in pictures or in sheer imagination or fantasy. They might even think of this as a safe way to get sexual feelings without risking a pregnancy or STIs. The main problem with masturbation is that such physical arousal and lustful imagination amounts to having awkward sex with an imagined someone who is not one's married spouse for life. That's why some churches count this as sin. Such imaginary one-flesh sex can get addicting.

From Ryan,

Some of my friends like to look at sexy pictures or videos for fun. Does the Bible say anything about this?

From Uncle Al,

Yes, it does. Sexually arousing pictures (or even sexually stimulating reading materials) are often part of

AT OUR HOUSE

1. **Discuss with your parents why porn is a serious issue.**
2. **Discuss with your parents the best way to deal with porn.**

such sexual experiences. This is called "pornography." Anyone who watches TV or movies, listens to contemporary music, or uses the Internet is likely to bump into pornography. It has many destructive effects, including undermining the one-flesh unifying mutual joy that God has beautifully designed you to enjoy with your future spouse when you get married. It leads a boy who watches porn to look at real girls and women as things, rather than people, things that can be used to get pleasure. When a girl watches porn the same happens in how she views boys or men. It's "a leading cause of marital and family breakdown today."[63] Kids who want to grow up emotionally and spiritually healthy in Christ run away from pornography every time they meet it. Just stop to think for one moment: Would you really want your future spouse to be masturbating and watching pornography right now? If not, then why would you want to do so now?[64]

When God beautifully designed Adam and Eve's bodies, He designed their brains to release oxytocin (sometimes called the "bonding hormone") each time they reached a sexual orgasm (or "climax") of intense pleasure. That happens best when a husband and wife have sex in a faithful genuinely loving covenant for life. In the 21st century, scientists who study human brains are learning how our brains change throughout our lives, especially how they change as a result of our choices and experiences. This is called "neuroplasticity."[65] Since our sexual choices and experiences are some of our most significant life experiences, these may change how our brains work more than most other experiences. Is this what Paul referred to in 1 Corinthians 6:18 quoted above?

Our brains change when we view pornography, where emotionally we become "one flesh" with strangers, most of whom are not normal real people. Actors shown in pornography are doing an act, pretending to be more happy than they really are. Most porn actors do it for the money and only for a year or two. Many porn actors are on drugs. Many have their bodies changed by surgeons to look more "sexy" than they are naturally. In short, porn is a lie.[66]

Printed pictures of porn stars are often electronically touched up to look more sexy than they actually look in real life. Kids and adults, both male and female, tend to get addicted to these fantasy images of what looks sexy, and so they are handicapped in relating to real mates in marriage. Sadly, pornography mostly shows sex acts without the committed loving relationship of a married husband and wife. But God beautifully designed us to have a committed loving husband-wife relationship in marriage, to make one-flesh sex acts a spiritual, emotional, and physical whole. Pornography often pushes the limits of what is even physically possible.[67] It makes people feel they can never measure up to what they see there. It gives them mental images they can never erase from their minds.

Also, pornography often excites people into trying the behaviours they have seen. Such experiments too often focus on the physical dimension of sexual intercourse, not on the emotional and spiritual union of a loving husband and wife who are committed to each other for life. That makes these adventures really quite counterfeit. In many ways, "porn kills love."[68] These are just a few of many reasons that kids who want to grow up healthy in Christ stay away from porn entirely.

From Ryan,

How should we deal with porn if we bump into it accidentally or with friends?

From Uncle Al,

When you use the Internet, unfortunately you will most likely bump into porn, either accidentally or by your choice, by yourself or with friends. That's an epidemic in our increasingly messed-up

AT OUR HOUSE

1. **Ask your parents what to do if a friend or a stranger tries to have sex with you or tries to touch you in unsafe ways.**
2. **Ask your parents what they think of masturbation and today's pornography**

world. In Jim Burns's *Purity Code* book and pledge he includes "turn my eyes from worthless things."[69] In *Good Pictures Bad Pictures*[70] a mom and dad teach their child *what* pornography is, *why* it's dangerous, and *how* to reject it. They recommend a "CAN DO plan" for kids who bump into porn: *Good Pictures Bad Pictures* includes an easy to remember 5-Point CAN DO Plan that teaches kids how to avoid pornography and minimize the troubling memories of accidental exposure. Let me recommend that you get a free CAN DO Plan poster pdf at their website www.ProtectYoungMinds.org. Porn runs on feelings, not on thinking, especially not on thinking about the Scriptures we discussed in Chapter 5.

Sadly, "comprehensive" sex ed programs in school too often prompt kids into trying the behaviours they have learned about. These programs too often focus on the physical dimension of sexual intercourse, not on the emotional and spiritual union of a loving husband and wife who are committed to each other for life. Some school comprehensive sex ed programs never once mention love or marriage. How "comprehensive" is that? Some even recommend that kids get further sex ed from the Internet, which often leads them into destructive porn addictions. Most fail to warn of the dangers discussed in Chapter 10.

AT OUR HOUSE

1. **Discuss with your parents the CAN DO plan for dealing with porn you encounter.**

10 IS SEX DANGEROUS?

(Caution: some issues in Chapters 8 to 11 may not be suitable for every 8- to 12-year-old tween.)

From Ryan,

Is it true that all sex is dangerous?

From Uncle Al,

No, Ryan, sex as God designed it for husband and wife in marriage is not dangerous. For most husbands and wives in a lifelong covenant marriage, sex is an exciting experience of expressing their abiding love for each other, as God wonderfully intended it to be for people He created in His image and for His greater glory.

But sex can be very dangerous for people who don't respect God's directions for its proper use in adulthood.

For example, some people think that everyone who has sex risks getting an STI. Dr. Grossman says no. "[T]he degree of risk depends not only on *what* you do, as students are taught, but on *who you do it with.*" (Emphasis is hers.) Then she adds,

> Students must know that men who have sex with men (MSM) [called homosexuals] and women and men who have sex with women and men (MSM/W) and (WSM/W) – commonly called bisexuals – are also vulnerable minorities. MSM is a population with a high prevalence of

> sexually transmitted infections, including HIV. This is related to risk behaviors that characterize this group: early age of sexual debut, high numbers of sexual partners, concurrent partners, infrequent condom use.
>
> The rate of new HIV diagnoses of men who have sex with men is 44 times that of other men and more than 40 times that of women; the rate of primary and secondary syphilis of men who have sex with men is 46 times that of other men and more than 71 times that of women. [71]

These medical scientific facts are not included in the NYC curriculum, nor are they included in most "comprehensive" sex ed programs in the world. Men having sex with men, and women and men having sex with women and men face major health risks, scientifically, quite apart from what any religions say about this. Our modern, politically correct secular media and educators simply refuse to say this, likely for fear of offending the LGBTQ (lesbian, gay, bisexual, transgendered, queer [some include intersex, and other categories]) community, which exercises political power totally out of proportion to its numbers of people in any country.

Yes, LGBTQ people exist in many parts of the world. Yes, some of them are hated, bullied, even murdered by others. That's always wrong. Yes, some of them commit suicide. That's always a tragedy. Why do they commit suicide? Likely some of them did so because they were hated, bullied, or not accepted as normal. Likely not all of them committed suicide for those reasons. Kids who want to grow up in Christ learn to *agape*-love and respect all people as

AT OUR HOUSE

1. **Discuss why secular media and schools usually fail to teach the sex science reported by WHO.**
2. **Discuss why secular media and schools usually fail to teach the sex science reported by Dr. Grossman.**

created in God's image, regardless of what messed-up ideas they believe, say, and do. That includes LGBTQ people.

From Ryan,

Does the Bible say anything about this?

From Uncle Al,

Yes, it does. We've already seen how God created Adam and Eve for "one-flesh" sexual unity by which they reflected God's image and procreated children.

After their 430 years of slavery in Egypt, it was rather difficult for newly freed Israelites and their fellow travellers to make "charitable judgments" about many Egyptian beliefs and behaviours. The same was true about many Canaanite beliefs and behaviours that the Israelites were about to meet in their new Promised Land. The same is true in parts of the New Testament that speak of the sexual practices out of which new Christians had been saved by faith in Christ.

The common sexual lifestyles we see in our world today that deviate from God's moral law in the Bible are surprisingly similar to the common deviant sexual lifestyles the children of Israel saw in their world of Egypt, Canaan, Babylon and which the early Christian church saw in the Roman Empire. Of course, we have electricity and its technology, engines, rockets, central heating, and better medicine. But our "politically correct" morality is surprisingly similar to that of the ancient world. Israel saw in the world of Egypt, Canaan, Babylon, and the early Christian church saw in the Roman Empire, examples of men having sexual experiences with other men and boys (homosexuality, pederasty [men having sex with boys], pedophilia [adults having sex with children]), women having sexual experiences with other women and girls (lesbianism, homosexuality, pedophilia), and both men and women having sexual experiences with their own kin (incest) and with animals (bestiality). All of these are prohibited in the Bible (as normally understood), because God wants His people to practise human sexuality as He designed it for humans' proper enjoyment and for pro-creating the next generation. Animals generally have no difficulties reproducing "after their kind" by instinct, even if the males of a few species like to poke their penises into holes other than female vaginas of their own kind. As created in God's image, humans are different from animals in that we have minds, souls, spirits, free will, imagination, moral choices, and many other unique abilities. We're not mere animals living by animal instincts.

For example, In Leviticus 18:1–3, 6, 20, 22–30 we read,

> Then the LORD said to Moses, "Give the following instructions to the people of Israel. I am the LORD your God. So *do not act like the people in Egypt,* where you used to live, or like the *people of Canaan,* where I am taking you. You must not imitate their way of life....
>
> "You must never have sexual relations with a *close relative*, for I am the LORD....
>
> "Do not defile yourself by having sexual intercourse with your *neighbor's wife....*
>
> "Do not practice *homosexuality,* having sex with another man as with a woman. It is a detestable sin. A man must not defile himself by having *sex with an animal*. And a woman must not offer herself to a male animal to have intercourse with it. This is a perverse act.
>
> "Do not defile yourselves in any of these ways, for the people I am driving out before you have defiled themselves in all these ways. Because the entire land has become defiled, I am punishing the people who live there. I will cause the *land to vomit them out....*
>
> "All these detestable activities are practiced by the people of the land where I am taking you, and *this is how the land has become defiled.* So do not defile the land and give it a reason to vomit you out, as it will vomit out the people who live there now. Whoever commits any of these detestable sins will be cut off from the community of Israel. So obey my instructions, and *do not defile* yourselves by committing any of these detestable practices that were committed by the people who lived in the land before you. I am the LORD your God." (Emphasis added.)

Observe the following notes on this passage:

1. It is clearly written in the context of common practices in Egypt and Canaan, calling God's people to be very different

from them in their sex ethics (v. 3), lest the land also vomit them out (v. 25–30).

2. The prohibition against incest is spelled out in great detail in verses 7–19 and 21. (Also see Leviticus 20:11–12, 17–21.)
3. The prohibition against adultery (v. 20) echoes the seventh commandment; it essentially prohibits all sex outside a lifelong marriage covenant (also see Leviticus 20:10). This flatly contradicts today's politically correct sex ethics that teaches, "If it feels good, do it – provided both partners are consenting adults or kids and they use protection."
4. The prohibition against homosexual (gay) sex is clearly spelled out in verse 22. (Also see Leviticus 20:13–14.)
5. The prohibition against bestiality (sex with animals) is clearly spelled out in verse 23. (Also see Leviticus 20:15–16.) Though this is not a major public issue in our time, it is reported occasionally in a various places.

Paul writes in Romans 1:21–32,

> Yes, they knew God, but they *wouldn't worship him as God* or even *give him thanks.* And they began to think up *foolish ideas* of what God was like. As a result, their *minds became dark and confused. Claiming to be wise,* they instead became *utter fools.* And instead of worshiping the glorious, ever-living God, they worshiped idols made to look like mere people and birds and animals and reptiles.
>
> So *God abandoned them to do whatever shameful things their hearts desired.* As a result, they did vile and degrading things with each other's bodies. They *traded the truth about God for a lie.* So they worshiped and served the things God created instead of the Creator himself, who is worthy of eternal praise! Amen. That is why *God abandoned them to their shameful desires.* Even the women turned *against the natural way* to have sex and instead indulged in sex with each other. And the men, instead of having normal sexual relations with women, *bumed with lust for each other.* Men did shameful things with other men, and as a result of this sin, they *suffered within themselves* the penalty they deserved.
>
> Since they thought it foolish to acknowledge God, he *abandoned them to their foolish thinking and let them do things that should never be done.* Their lives became full of every kind of wickedness, sin, greed, hate, envy, murder, quarreling, deception, malicious behavior, and gossip. They are backstabbers, haters of God, insolent, proud, and boastful. They *invent new ways of sinning*, and

> they disobey their parents. They refuse to understand, break their promises, are heartless, and have no mercy. They know God's justice requires that those who do these things deserve to die, yet they *do them anyway.* Worse yet, they *encourage others to do them, too.* (Emphasis added.)

Observe the following notes on this passage:

1. This sinful gay behaviour comes up when people reject God, sometimes worshipping idols instead, and when people are unthankful (v. 21).
2. Though these people think they are wise, God calls these ideas "foolish" and the people "fools" for believing and living them (v. 21–23, 28). They traded God's truth for a lie (v. 25).
3. As punishment for their sin, God lets them do what they want (v. 24, 26).
4. Women having sex with women (lesbian sex) and men having sex with men (gay sex) is unnatural, or against natural law (v .26–27); that is, it violates the way God created men and women sexually (Genesis 2:20–24).
5. Gay and lesbian sex brings suffering (v. 27).
6. Gay and lesbian sex brings many other sins (v. 29–31).
7. Gays and lesbians encourage others to join them in their destructive lifestyles, even if they know it's wrong (v. 32).

Paul also writes in 1 Corinthians 6:9–20,

> Don't you realize that those who *do wrong will not inherit the Kingdom of God*? Don't fool yourselves. Those who indulge in sexual sin, or who *worship idols,* or commit *adultery*, or are *male prostitutes,* or practice *homosexuality,* or are *thieves,* or *greedy* people, or *drunkards*, or are *abusive,* or *cheat* people – *none of these will inherit the Kingdom of God. Some of you were once like that.* But you were cleansed; you were made holy; *you were made right with God* by calling on the name of the Lord Jesus Christ and by the Spirit of our God.
>
> You say, "I am allowed to do anything" – but *not everything is good for you.* And even though "I am allowed to do anything," *I must not become a slave to anything.* You say, "Food was made for the stomach, and the stomach for food." (This is true, though someday God will do away with both of them.) But *you can't say that our bodies were made for sexual immorality.* They were *made for the Lord,* and the *Lord cares about our bodies.* And God will raise us

> from the dead by his power, just as he raised our Lord from the dead.
> Don't you realize that *your bodies are actually parts of Christ*? Should a man take his body, which is part of Christ, and *join it to a prostitute? Never!* And don't you realize that if a man joins himself to a prostitute, *he becomes one body with her*? For the Scriptures say, "The two are united into one." But the person who is joined to the Lord is one spirit with him.
> Run from sexual sin! *No other sin so clearly affects the* body as this one does. For sexual immorality is a *sin against your own body.* Don't you realize that *your body is the temple of the Holy Spirit,* who lives in you and was given to you by God? *You do not belong to yourself, for God bought you with a high price.* So you must *honor God with your body.* (Emphasis added.)

Observe the following notes on this passage:

1. "[T]hose who do wrong will not inherit the Kingdom of God" (v. 9)
2. Gay sex is listed with many other sins (v. 9–10).
3. Paul observes that some Corinthian Christians "were once like that. But you were cleansed; you were made holy; you were made right with God," (v. 11). Note that gays can and do change, even if "in their minds it feels like they were born that way."[72] The belief that LGBTQ people were born that way and can never change gives them the feeling that they are entitled to say and do what they "are" without criticism or

AT OUR HOUSE

1. **Compare how differently Israel's views of our bodies and sex were to be from those of Egypt and Canaan.**
2. **Compare how differently Christians' views of our bodies and sex are to be from those of the world around us.**

Bonus: For one week, try to keep a record of events that show how the world around us has a different view of our bodies and sex from what the Bible teaches. Then discuss your list with your parents or another mature Christian adult.

consequences.

4. Even on food issues, those who say, "I am allowed to do anything," Paul cautions "but not everything is good for you" (v. 12).
5. Paul then adds, "But you can't say that our bodies were made for sexual immorality. They were made for the Lord, and the Lord cares about our bodies" (v. 13). Only in Christianity is there such importance placed on our bodies, their sexual purity, and on God's care about them as actual parts of Christ (v. 15).
6. A Christian who has a one-flesh sexual union with anyone besides a spouse, as in prostitution, is seriously violating the one-flesh union of husband and wife. A Christian must be joined in spiritual union only with Christ and a married sexually complementary spouse, no one else (v. 15–17). People who enter one-flesh sexual unions with several people tend to mess themselves up physically, emotionally, and spiritually, because God did not design us for such behaviour. A Christian must run from it (v. 18) for many sound reasons, including that it's a "sin against your own body."
7. We don't belong to ourselves, to do anything we want with our bodies. God bought us with Christ's shed blood to be a temple of the Holy Spirit to be a place where God is glorified (v.19-20).

Paul also writes in 1 Timothy 1:8–11,

> We know that the *law is good when used correctly*. For the law was not intended for people who do what is right. It is for people who are lawless and rebellious, who are ungodly and sinful, who consider nothing sacred and defile what is holy, who kill their father or mother or commit other murders. The *law is for people who are sexually immoral,* or who practice *homosexuality*, or are *slave traders, liars, promise breakers, or who do anything else that contradicts the wholesome teaching that comes from the glorious Good News entrusted to me by our blessed God.* (Emphasis added.)

Observe the following notes on this passage:

1. Even in the New Testament age of grace, there is a good correct way to use God's moral law to point out the wrong done by rebellious, ungodly sinners (v. 8–9).
2. These people are lawless in many ways, including how they misuse sex (v. 9–10).
3. Whole healthy people normally do what is right by God's standards (v. 11).

From Brook,

When the Bible talks about men having sex with men, what does that mean? Can you help us sort some of the facts from myths about this?

From Ms. Barb,

Let me try, Brook. WebMD.com reports, "An estimated 90 percent of men who have sex with men and as many as 5 percent to 10 percent of sexually active women engage in receptive anal intercourse."[73] That is, they let a man insert his penis in the receiver's anus, which is part of the body's digestive system, not part of the body's reproductive system. WebMD.com adds, "There are serious health risks with this practice."[74] Besides serious risk for HIV from anal sex, studies show that such exposure to the human papillomavirus (HPV) may also lead to the development of anal warts and anal cancer, with and without using condoms.

In Dr. Grossman's *You're Teaching My Child What?* she devotes 15 pages to this subject, because it is normally not treated in secular "comprehensive" sex ed programs.[75] She includes the quote from former US Surgeon General, C. Everett Koop: "Condoms provide some protection, but anal intercourse is simply too dangerous to practice."[76] Dr. Grossman agrees heartily.

Egale Canada Human Rights Trust is Canada's leading LGBTQ activist group. In May 2015 they ran TV ads announcing that LGBTQ youth commit suicide at four times the rate of other youth. Their 2013 survey showed that 33 percent of LGBTQ youth have attempted suicide compared to 7 percent of other youth.[77] How many secular "comprehensive" sex ed programs report such data to students?

From Brook,

What does "oral sex" mean? Can you help us sort some of the facts from myths about this?

From Ms. Barb,

Quite simply, "oral sex" is any sexual activity that involves contact between one partner's mouth and a partner's genitals. WebMD.com reports, "Several sexually transmitted diseases (STDs), including HIV, herpes, syphilis, gonorrhea, HPV, and viral hepatitis can be passed on through oral sex."[78] Because the girl cannot get pregnant through oral sex, this happens more often among some tweens and teens than vaginal sex (where the boy's penis enters the girl's vagina). But that does not mean that oral sex is safe, either physically or emotionally. Besides the risks of getting STIs, neither partner can predict reliably how they will feel about such events at any time in the future. Sadly, most secular sex ed programs treat vaginal, oral, and anal sex as quite similar sexual behaviour.[79] That is scientifically irresponsible. Dr. Grossman notes that the risks can be up to a million-fold different, depending on the particular oral sex practise.[80] Many online "sexpert" sites promote oral sex as safe. The US National Center for Health Statistics found that only nine percent of teens practising oral sex were using condoms.[81]

AT OUR HOUSE

1. **Compare how differently Christians' views of sex are to be from sex ed programs in school.**
2. **Compare how differently Christians' views of LGBTQ activities are to be from sex ed programs in school.**

Dr. Grossman also warns that promiscuous people (those

who have sex with multiple partners), both teens and adults,[82] routinely lie about their previous sex experiences and their STI status. We've already noted above that many STIs show no symptoms for some time. That means that infected sex partners can transmit STIs to others without even knowing they were infected.

From Ryan,

If LGBTQ people have sex with someone who is the same sex they are, is that normal?

From Uncle Al,

Let's, first make some words clear. Women who like to have sexual experiences with women are called "lesbian" (or "gay") and men who like to have sexual experiences with men are called "gay." Both are called "homosexual."[83] Men and women who like to have any kind of sexual experiences with both men and women are called "bisexual." Men and women who like to have any kind of sexual experiences only with someone of the opposite sex (for example, as in a husband-and-wife covenant marriage) are called "straight" or "heterosexual." Men who really feel they should be women, and women who really feel they should be men, are called "transgendered." Men and women who are really not sure with whom they like to have any kind of sexual experiences are called "queer." Whether someone thinks of themselves as straight, lesbian, gay, bisexual, transgendered, or queer (LGBTQ) is called that person's "sexual orientation." These terms have entered our common public language in recent decades at the insistence of the LGBTQ activists. However, the LGBTQ activists insist that all sexual orientations are a normal part of every culture around our globe and have been throughout human history.

From Ryan,

Some of my friends say that gays are born that way and can

never change. Is that true? Some say being gay is a choice. Is that true? How many people are gay?

From Uncle Al,

LGBTQ activists insist that all people are born with their sexual orientation and can never actually change. This belief then entitles them to say and do what they want sexually without criticisms or consequences. Many scholars reject that idea as false. In fact, except when someone is raped, each time someone has sex with someone else, both partners have made a choice about that event. So it's a choice to do gay sex acts, but it's not a choice to be tempted to do gay sex acts.

It's not sin to be tempted about anything. Jesus has been tempted in every way, just as we are—yet he did not sin (**Hebrews 4:15,** NIV). So Jesus may well have been tempted to have sex with a woman, not his wife, (that is, Jesus may well have been tempted to commit adultery) and He may well have been tempted to have sex with a man (that is, Jesus may well have been tempted to do gay sex acts). It's not sin to be tempted to have sex with either your sex or with someone of the opposite sex, because you do not choose to be tempted (though you may choose to do things and go places where you are likely to be tempted). But it is sin to have sex with someone to whom you are not married, and it is sin to marry someone of your same sex. If someone is tempted to have sex with someone of their same sex, that is no reason to conclude "I must be gay" any more than if someone is tempted to have sex with someone of the opposite sex to conclude "I must be straight." We are tempted without our choice. We act on those temptations by our choice, either to yield to the temptations or to resist them in the power of the Holy Spirit.

Kids who want to grow up in Christ prefer to self-identify as "I am a beloved follower of King Jesus!" They have no need to wonder if they are straight or gay. Some 98 percent of tweens and teens are naturally attracted to someone of the opposite sex, unless they mess themselves up with too many thoughts of "Am I gay?" It's really not smart to get too focused on such questions, in spite of what others urge on us.

How many people are gay? In fact, some report that the number of ex-gays are more than the total number of gays and bisexuals combined.[84] New Zealand government scientific researcher Neil Whitehead writes, "About half of the homosexual/bisexual population (in a non-therapeutic environment) moves towards heterosexuality over a lifetime. About 3 percent of the present heterosexual population once firmly believed themselves to be homosexual or bisexual. Sexual orientation is not set in concrete."[85] Psychologist Stanton Jones reports that the "best contemporary scientific findings are that when one identical twin brother is gay, the probabilities of the second twin being gay are approximately 10 percent."[86]

Since identical twins have identical genes or DNA, one would expect that if one of them is gay, then the other one should be gay too, if it were true that gays are born that way and can never actually change. However, in a 2000 study in Australia, only 11 percent of male and 14 percent of female co-twins were both gay. In a 2002 study in the US only 7.7 percent of male and 5.3 percent of female co-twins were both gay.[87] You need not expect to be told such medical science in secular school "comprehensive" sex ed classes.

How many people express the LGBTQ sexual orientations? "Based on the 2013 NHIS data, 96.6 percent of adults identified as straight, 1.6 percent identified as gay or lesbian, and 0.7 percent identified as bisexual. The remaining 1.1 percent of adults identified as 'something else,' stated 'I don't know the answer,' or refused to provide an answer."[88] An article in *The Atlantic* says, "The Williams Institute at UCLA School of Law, a gay and lesbian think tank, released a study in April 2011 estimating based on its research that just 1.7 percent of Americans between 18 and 44 identify as gay or lesbian, while another 1.8 percent – predominantly women – identify as bisexual."[89]

From Brook,

What do the LGBTQ people say about how many people express the LGBTQ sexual preferences?

From Ms. Barb,

This is an interesting area of debate. In 1948 Alfred Kinsey published a study of sexual practices reported by American men. In 1953 he published a similar study of sexual practices reported by American women. Many gay activists have argued that these data show that 10 percent of Americans are gay or bisexual. That number has been commonly reported ever since. The problem is that Kinsey interviewed a biased sample of reform school students, prisoners, male prostitutes, and other volunteers from gay groups. That method is neither fair nor scientific.[90] Gay activists have a clear agenda: They want everyone to agree that sex outside marriage is normal.[91] Exaggerating their numbers seems to be part of their strategy toward this goal.

In 2011 Egale Canada published *Every Class in Every School*, based on a survey of over 3,700 Grade 7 to 12 students across Canada. It reported that 14.1 percent of these students described themselves as LGBTQ (though Statistics Canada found only 1.3% of the population between 18 to 59 years identified as homosexual [lesbian and gay] in 2012, and only 1.1% identified as bisexual). Since the focus of this study was to document how LGBTQ students are bullied, in recruiting these survey respondents the team of researchers "implemented an open-access online survey and advertised it widely through news releases and website and Facebook notices and by systematically contacting every organization across the country that we identified as having

AT OUR HOUSE

1. **Ask your parents what they think of those who show hate to gays and why.**
2. **Ask your parents whether they think people can change sexual preferences.**

LGBTQ youth membership."[92] Such research methods using volunteers are often criticized as using "convenience samples" or "snowball sampling." Their findings do not fairly represent the general populations of any country or professional group.

Many Christians believe that secular sex education without a biblical theological context does kids a disservice and prompts more premature mutual exploration and experimentation, to the detriment of most kids. Small wonder that sexually transmitted infections and unwanted pregnancies tripled in the first decade or two of the new secular sex education programs of the 1970s and '80s. Small wonder that Egale Canada's 2011 study provided the "scientific" rationale for Ontario's Bill 13 (2012), Manitoba's Bill 18 (2013), and Alberta's Bill 10 (2015), which mandated that every school, public and private, where one or more students requested a Gay-Straight Alliance, must accommodate such a student club, thereby declaring that "gay is okay." Logically, if it is true that gay behaviour really is okay, then anyone who says that gay behaviour really is not okay would be wrong. But we've already seen above that the Bible clearly teaches that gay behaviour really is not okay.

What the Egale study (and others like it) fail to show is how much teens change in their feelings about their sexual attractions. In 2014 family doctor David van Gend, head of the Australian Marriage Forum wrote, "Is the gay bullying plague in schools a myth?" He sent it as an open letter to the Australian education minister. He questioned the wisdom of the Australian Education Union's 2006 gender identity policy, which declares that "homosexuality, bisexuality, transgenderism and intersex need to be normalised." Dr. van Gend suggested that gay-straight alliances in schools may do more harm than good because these may draw more tweens and teens to believe they were born gay and cannot change, while gay behaviour is significantly unhealthy, including increased risks for depression and suicide. He cites many studies around the world, including the American College of Pediatricians report:

> Adolescence is well recognized for its sexual fluidity

> and instability of homosexual attractions. In 2007, Savin-Williams and Ream conducted a large longitudinal study that documented changes in attraction so great between the ages of 16 and 17 that they questioned whether the concept of sexual orientation had any meaning for adolescents with homosexual attractions. Seventy-five percent of adolescents who had some initial homosexual attraction between the ages of 17–21 changed to experience heterosexual attraction only.
>
> This is in stark contrast to the stability they found among adolescents experiencing heterosexual attractions. Among these adolescents, fully 98 percent retained their heterosexual-only attractions into adulthood. Another study demonstrating significant change away from homosexual attractions in adolescence involved 13,840 youth. Of those initially "unsure" of their sexual orientation, 66 percent became exclusively heterosexual.[93]

Unfortunately, "comprehensive" sex education courses in schools usually fail to report such data.

From Ryan,

My friend says that being "transgender" is okay. What does this mean? Is the Bible okay with this?

From Uncle Al,

Remember that all humans are sinners and all nature has been cursed by sin, so that we all live in a very messed-up world (**Romans 3:23; 8:20-21**). That includes the fact that on rare occasions some people, including some kids, may experience periods of confusion about themselves on any number of issues, including who God wants them to have sex with and when, or even who they really "are" as people sexually. Some such emotional confusions may last a long time, some are shorter. When we experience such confusions ourselves or encounter them in others, we need to respond very compassionately in *agape*-love with whoever is dealing with them. Biblically "transgenders" are as much created in God's image as all other people and therefore worthy of our *agape*-love and respect, certainly never of hate, shame, insults, or bullying of any sort.

The word "transgender" means "a person appearing or attempting to be a member of the opposite sex, as a transsexual or habitual cross-dresser."[94] This term has entered our language more widely in the 1990s. It has led to considerable debate in many circles, including laws that protect every person in the use of bathrooms, lockers, change rooms, and showers devoted to the sex with which they now identify or feel comfortable. In play some boys like to pretend to be girls and some girls like to pretend to be boys. That's harmless fun.

But some biological girls are really unsure what they emotionally "feel" they "are" sexually, regardless of their bodies and how they were born. Also, some biological boys are really unsure what they emotionally "feel" they "are" sexually. Such "gender identity confusion" (or "gender dysphoria"[95] as the APA calls it) has prompted Facebook to ask new people who register with them whether they are male or female or "other," and offer over 50 options for the last category. Note how feelings become more important than one's actual body here. One website lists 113 genders.[96]

The secular periodical *LiveScience* quotes Lynn Carr: "Sex is the biological (that is, male/female); gender is the social (for example, masculine, feminine, androgynous [both male and female or neither[97]]); sexuality is the erotic (for example, heterosexual, bisexual, homosexual, autosexual [preferring self-gratification[98]], celibate)."[99] Regardless of which gender they prefer as their sex partner Carr says, many people resent having to conform to the stereotypes of their gender.

In **Genesis 1:27, 28; 2:21— 25** we read:

> So God created human beings in his own image. In the image of God he created them; male and female he created them. Then God

> blessed them and said, "Be fruitful and multiply. Fill the earth and govern it... So the LORD God caused the man to fall into a deep sleep. While the man slept, the LORD God took out one of the man's rib and closed up the opening. Then the LORD God made a woman from the rib, and he brought her to the man. "At last!" the man exclaimed. "This one is bone from my bone, and flesh from my flesh! She will be called 'woman,' because she was taken from 'man.'" This explains why a man leaves his father and mother and is joined to his wife, and the two are united into one. Now the man and his wife were both naked, but they felt no shame.

There may be no hint of "transgender" in the Bible or ancient cultures.

Before the 1990s, girls who preferred to doing "boyish" stuff (for example, climbing trees, wrestling, playing with tractors and trucks, and so on) were considered "tomboys," and boys who preferred to doing "girly" stuff (for example, playing with dolls, caring for babies, cooking, sewing, and so on) were considered "pansies" or "moma's boys." (Actually, it's fine for both boys and girls to enjoy both kinds of activities.) Now it has become fashionable with some parents and doctors to give such kids hormones and prepare them for "sex-change" surgeries to make them look like the sex opposite to the sex with which they were born – all in hopes that their feelings of "gender identity" will improve. But, all such hormones and "sex-change" surgeries do not change the male or female chromosomes in each of the 37 trillion cells in the "transgendered" person's body.[100] A transgender fad rapidly spreading in UK primary schools, shows 'clusters' emerging as children copy their transgender friends.[101] Some say this movement means reality has now died in our culture.[102]

AT OUR HOUSE

1. **Ask your parents how they respond to "transgender" laws.**
2. **Ask your parents how they respond to using non-prescription drugs.**

However, a growing number of these people later regret having done these changes, because they are more emotionally pained with their new "gender" than they were previously, besides the fact that they can never pro-create kids after such surgeries, even if they get married. Sy Rogers was scheduled for his "sex-change" surgery in the 1970s, but in a spiritual awakening he changed his mind before the surgery. He has helped many other troubled "transgenders" since. He reports that he personally knows four women who became men and six men who became women; all ten reversed back to their birth gender identities and behaviours.[103]

A recent study of 6,450 transgenders showed why so many regret their "sex-change" surgeries, including 41% who attempted suicide.[104] In the 1970s Johns Hopkins Hospital was the leading US hospital that did "sex-change" surgery. But then they stopped. Its former psychiatrist-in-chief Dr. Paul R. McHugh, in 2014 wrote in the *Wall Street Journal* that transgenderism is a "mental disorder" that merits treatment, and that sex change is "biologically impossible."[105] McHugh said that people who promote sexual reassignment surgery are collaborating with and promoting a mental disorder[106] (gender dysphoria) and that among people who had reassignment surgery the suicide rate is 20 times higher than among non-transgender people. McHugh further noted studies from Vanderbilt University and London's Portman Clinic of children who had expressed transgender feelings but for whom, over time, 70 to 80 percent "spontaneously lost those feelings" as they grew up. McHugh said "People who undergo sex-reassignment surgery do not change from men to women or vice versa. Rather, they become feminized men or masculinized women."[107] "The American College of Pediatricians urges educators and legislators to reject all policies that condition children to accept as normal a life of chemical and surgical impersonation of the opposite sex. Facts – not ideology – determine reality."[108] Small wonder that secular media and secular schools tend not to report such scientific data and opinions.

Small wonder that secular governments seek to show their compassion for these people by passing laws to protect their "rights" to use any bathroom, change room or shower where they feel comfortable. Sadly, such protections ignore how uncomfortable girls and women are with meeting transgendered boys and men in their women's bathrooms, change rooms or showers. Many consider policies that welcome transgendered boys and men in their women's bathrooms, change rooms or showers to be an open invitation to predators to pretend to be transgendered, so they can enter women's bathrooms, change rooms or showers to take pictures, assault, or rape girls and women there. Such crimes have already happened. For such victims this kind of unwanted sex is dangerous. Laws and policies that are meant to protect the transgenders, but that fail to protect others, are also dangerous.

Sadly, too often transgenders are bullied mercilessly. Some people joke that transgenders can be recognized by a close look at their Adam's apple or their hands. Kids who follow Christ never bully anyone or tease or shame anyone about anything, because that might hurt them. Feelings matter and words can hurt. *Agape*-love and respect are always proper for every person because God created them in His image and sent Christ to die for their sin. Kids who follow Christ know their identity is as beloved children of God who have crucified their sinful lusts.

11 ARE SOME CHRISTIANS GAY?

(Caution: some issues in Chapters 8–11 may not be suitable for every 8- to 12 year-old tween.)

From Brook,

My friend said that some Christians are gay. What do you say about this?

From Ms. Barb,

Yes, some liberal evangelical Christians argue that they or some others were born gay and can never change their sexual orientation (preference for sex partners), so they are equally entitled to same-sex sex is in a faithful monogamous (only one sex partner) "marriage." They argue that God does not want most people to go through life single (Genesis 2:18: "It is not good for the man to be alone"), and since LGBTQ people (lesbians, gays, bisexuals, transgendered, queers) are not exclusively attracted to people of the opposite sex, they can never look forward to a husband-and-wife marriage, and that's not fair. Some liberal evangelical Christians argue that all the Bible passages we looked at above don't actually show that the sexual practices of faithful monogamous "married" LGBTQ couples are wrong. They argue that these passages only talk about people having gay sex in the context of idolatry, or with children too young to give informed consent, or that Old Testament (OT) laws don't apply to New Testament (NT) Christians in this age of grace . Some even argue that none of the Bible writers knew anything of sexual orientation as we do today. So they argue that faithful monogamous marriage of Bible-believing lesbians and gays is okay, because the Bible actually says nothing about that. They also argue that since Jesus said nothing about LGBTQ sexual behaviour, it must be okay.[109]

However, historian N. T. Wright says,

> One thing that I do know, as an ancient historian, is that there is nothing in contemporary understanding and experience of homosexual condition and behavior that was unknown in the first century. The idea that in the first century it was all about masters having odd relationships with slaves, or older men with younger men – yeah, sure, that happened – but read Plato's *Symposium*. They have permanent, faithful, stable male-male partnerships, lifelong stuff – Achilles and Patroclus in Homer, all sorts of things….
>
> Paul in Corinth will not have been unaware, in a world where private life only is for the very rich and the very aristocratic, everyone else does what they do pretty much in public. Paul will have known the full range of stuff, so that the idea that "Oh, well, in the first century they didn't know, we now with our scientific knowledge" – that's a little bit of Enlightenment arrogance again actually.[110]

He adds that most men may like to have sex with many women. But that does not mean they should, or that they can't control such urges.

Philosopher Hendrik van der Breggen comments,

> Thus, even though ancient philosophers and Bible writers didn't know all we know scientifically about sexual orientation, it's reasonable to think that the ancients and Bible writers did know about homosexual orientation as a human condition, they knew about same-sex sexual

> behaviour, and they knew the difference between the two.[111]

Evangelist Ravi Zacharias was born in India, where he also spent his youth. He observes,

> The reason we are against racism is because a person's race is sacred,... you cannot violate it,... and the reason we react against the issue of homosexuality the way we do is because a person's sexuality is sacred too, you cannot violate it.... Sex is a sacred gift of God.... I can no longer justify an aberration of it in somebody else's life than I can justify my proclivities to go beyond my marital boundaries.... A disposition or a proclivity does not justify expressing that disposition or proclivity. That goes for all sexuality.[112]

It's not loving to tell anyone that they are free to do what they want for any reason.

From Ryan,

My Christian friend said that some gay Christians are celibate. What does that mean and what do you say about this?

From Uncle Al,

Yes, some conservative evangelical Christians argue that they or others were born gay and can never change their sexual orientation (preference for sex partners), so for them the biblical choice is to live the rest of their lives without ever having sex with anyone (that is, being celibate). The problem with this view is that we're all sinners, and any Christian who calls him or herself a "celibate gay Christian" is saying that their preference for same-sex partners is a cross they have to bear all their lives, from which they can never be delivered. That's not the view of the transforming power of God's Holy Spirit that the Bible teaches.[113]

From Brook,

What might I say to a friend who argues that "Jesus said nothing about LGBTQ behaviour, so it must be okay"?

From Ms. Barb,

You might say that yes, Jesus said nothing about LGBTQ sexual behaviour (at least nothing that's recorded in the New Testament). He also said nothing about incest or rape or sex with animals. Are those okay too? Hardly. Jesus said a lot about the Old Testament. He clearly said it was God's Word, to be obeyed. In Matthew 5 Jesus said,

> "Don't misunderstand why I have come. I did not come to abolish the law of Moses or the writings of the prophets. No, I came to accomplish their purpose. I tell you the truth, until heaven and earth disappear, not even the smallest detail of God's law will disappear until its purpose is achieved. So if you ignore the least commandment and teach others to do the same, you will be called the least in the Kingdom of Heaven. But anyone who obeys God's laws and teaches them will be called great in the Kingdom of Heaven.

And what did Jesus say about sex? Look what He said in Matthew 19:

> Some Pharisees came and tried to trap him with this question: "Should a man be allowed to divorce his wife for just any reason?"
> "Haven't you read the Scriptures?" Jesus replied. "They record that from the beginning 'God made them male and female.'" And he said, "'This explains why a man leaves his father and mother and is joined to his wife, and the two are united into one.' Since they are no longer two but one, let no one split apart what God has joined together."
> "Then why did Moses say in the law that a man could give his wife a written notice of divorce and send her away?" they asked.
> Jesus replied, "Moses permitted divorce only as a concession to your hard hearts, but it was not what God had originally intended.
> And I tell you this, whoever divorces his wife and marries someone else commits adultery – unless his wife has been unfaithful."

For Jesus, sex, as God designed it, is always only between a married husband and wife. Period.[114] Of some 31,000 verses in the Bible, not one of them has anything positive to say about LGBTQ sexual behaviour.

Yes, some OT laws don't apply to NT Christians. We've already seen how Hebrews shows that the OT ceremonial laws (about tabernacle and temple sacrifice, and so on) were fulfilled by Christ so they don't apply to NT Christians. The OT also has many civil laws that don't apply to NT Christians who don't live in the OT nation of Israel. Among many examples are the taboo against eating shellfish, tattoos, sowing mixed seeds in a field, or wearing clothes of mixed fabrics. These practices carried religious meaning in Canaanite religion that are not relevant to our culture. For example, in Canaanite religion sowing mixed seeds in a field or wearing clothes of mixed fabrics were believed to prompt their gods to have more sex, and so these gods would bless their fields with bigger crops. Today liberals and atheists like to make fun of the Bible as a silly book that no smart person believes anymore, because of such laws that seem silly to us. Such mocking of Christians who still believe the Bible is God's Word just shows how uniformed these liberals and atheists are about the history and the cultural context of the OT nation of Israel.

True compassion does not embrace the false beliefs and wrong behaviours of LGBTQ people, whether or not they call themselves Christians or say they believe the Bible. Also true compassion does not fear and loathe LGBTQ people and write off their souls wholesale. Such "homophobia" is sin.[115] Sadly, most LGBTQ people blame their own brokenness on the stigma they face from others who don't embrace their beliefs and behaviours. Some LGBTQ people (but not all) are very angry about that. But many LGBTQ people and their allies really believe that today every educated person must agree that LGBTQ behaviours are okay and normal. Where same-sex marriage is legal (now some 18 countries of our world's 200 countries), often LGBTQ people and their allies really believe that it is illegal discrimination for anyone to still believe that sexual experiences of any sort are morally right only between a married husband and wife, as God designed us, and to say so in public and make choices according to that belief. Misplaced compassion ("soft love") withholds God's truth. True *agape*-love tells the truth (Ephesians 4:15), whether or not that's popular. We need to accept all people as they are, even if we don't approve what they believe and do. We need to treat them with love and grace, whether or not they continue LGBTQ beliefs and behaviours, because like they, we too are messed-up sinners whether or not we have accepted Christ's forgiveness.

From Brook,

So how should I respond to my friend who says it's wrong to think that LGBTQ behaviours are not okay or normal for some?

From Ms. Barb,

With *agape*-love and respect. That's because all people are created in God's image, but we all are also messed-up sinners. It's so natural and easy to get irritated or angry at thieves, greedy people, drunkards, people who are abusive, cheaters, or people who practice homosexuality (1 Corinthians 6:9–10). But if you really want to grow up in Christ you will learn to practice *agape*-love and respect for all people because they are created in God's image, even those who support LGBTQ behaviours as being okay. Sadly, some parents or other family members or friends of people who "come out" as LGBTQ have behaved very unlovingly to them. That's wrong too. We need to treat all sinners with *agape*-love and respect, even as we urge them to "Go and sin no more," as Jesus told the woman caught in the act of adultery (John 8).

AT OUR HOUSE

1. **Discuss how to deal with being called a "hateful homophobic bigot."**
2. **Ask your parents how they respond to "silly" OT laws.**
3. **Ask whether your parents think Jesus said nothing about gay sex.**

Usually thieves know that it's wrong to steal, and adulterers know their adultery is wrong. Sadly, many gays have convinced themselves that for them gay sex is right because God made them that way and they can never change their gay sexual preferences. However, many ex-gays have reported that even during their years of gay behaviours, even gladly joining in many gay pride events, down deep they actually knew that their gay sexual preferences and behaviours were wrong. Thieves know that they choose to steal. Adulterers know that they choose to commit adultery. Yet gays say they have no choice about being gay, because that is who they "are." Does this make sense? Each person who engages in a sex act, makes a choice to do so. That does not mean that is who they "are." It means it is what they "do," even if they believe it is who they "are."

Ironically, the really challenging part can be how we respond to pro-LGBTQ people who angrily call us "hateful homophobic religious bigots" for believing that God created Adam and Eve for "one-flesh" unity sexually and that sex experiences should be saved only for our married spouses of the opposite sex. Sadly, some Bible-believing Christians have expressed hate for LGBTQ people, including members of their own family. That's sin. But God *agape*-loves "the world" (John 3:16), and so must we. However, that does not mean that we should believe that thieves, greedy people, drunkards, abusive people, cheaters, or people who practice homosexuality are right about what they believe and do. We need to learn to *agape*-love and respect them too, even while we disagree with what they believe and do. In fact, if we really *agape*-love and respect thieves, greedy people and drunkards, shouldn't we urge them to change their destructive behaviours? Shouldn't we do the same for abusive people, cheaters, or people who practice homosexuality? What is hateful about that? If they don't like that we disagree, does that mean we hate them? No, not necessarily.

And what is a "homophobic bigot"? A "bigot" is "a person who is utterly intolerant of any differing creed, belief, or opinion."[116] A "homophobe" is "a person who fears or hates homosexuals and homosexuality." Question: If we believe that sex outside a husband-and-wife marriage is wrong, does that make us "homophobic bigots"?[117] The politically correct world says yes. But if we agree with the Bible when it says that homosexual behaviours are violations of God's moral law, does that make us homophobic bigots, especially if we clearly *agape*-love and respect homosexuals as much as we do thieves, greedy people, drunkards, abusive people, or cheaters? That's what God does. He sent His own Son Jesus to die for the forgiveness of everyone who accepts His free gift of forgiveness. Sadly, there are some mentally ill "homophobes" who suffer from irrational fears of homosexuals.[118] Most Bible-believing Christians are not mentally ill, even if they believe that LGBTQ behaviours are wrong.

If you and I tolerate people with beliefs different from ours, then we are not bigots, even if we believe they are wrong. If you and I don't hate or fear homosexuals and homosexuality, then we are not homophobic, even if we believe they like to do wrong acts. Our problem is that most politically correct people don't understand this. Instead, they think that if we do not believe that gay is okay, then we are homophobic bigots. They seem to think that calling us such insulting names will shame us into agreeing with them. But calling anyone insulting names is not a form of reasonable discussion in search of truth. Rather, it's a form of bullying.[119] So it's especially important that kids who really want to grow up in Christ never call anyone insulting names or bully anyone for any reason. God loves them and so must we.

From Ryan,

My friend says that LGBTQ sex has been scientifically proven to be okay. What can I say about this?

From Uncle Al,

The American Psychiatric Association (APA) used to say that gays and lesbians were suffering from a mental illness, but in 1973 they stopped saying this. Perhaps your friend thinks that not defining it as an illness makes it "okay." The problem is that this change was not made on the basis of new scientific evidence.[120] Instead, it was made in response to a major political campaign by very dedicated gay activists, including some bullying and deception.[121] Such tactics have since convinced most professional societies and many western governments, scholars, and journalists to agree that gay is okay. However, the many attempts to show scientifically that gays and lesbians are born that way have all failed. LGBTQ historian David Benkof writes, "Being gay is in the software of some people's lives, but it's in nobody's hardware."[122] Some surveys of small select groups of gay and lesbian parents have concluded that their kids are okay, but other larger studies of adult children of gay and lesbian parents have concluded that their kids are more troubled on many issues than are adult children of normal mom-and-dad [husband-and-wife] parents.[123]

In a 2010 letter to school superintendents, Dr. Tom Benton, president of the American College of Pediatricians, wrote,

> There is no scientific evidence that an individual is born "gay" or "transgender." Instead, the best available research points to multiple factors – primarily social and familial – that predispose children and adolescents to homosexual attraction and/or gender confusion.... The longer students delay self-labeling as "gay," the less likely they are to experience these health risks. In fact, for each year an adolescent delays, the risk of suicide alone decreases by 20 percent.[124]

Dr. David Kyle Foster of Pure Passion was an active gay (had sex with over 1,000 men) for 10 years and now has not practised that lifestyle for over three decades. His view of how homosexual desire arises is that it is "born from a complicated convergence of our fallen nature, idolatry, rebellion, temperament, environment, experiences and developmental factors."[125]

In 2009 the *Journal of Human Sexuality* published a 128-page study report, "What Research Shows: The NARTH Response to the APA Claims on Homosexuality." Among its several conclusions, was the following:

> Over a century of experiential evidence, clinical reports, and research evidence demonstrate that it is possible for both men and women to change from homosexuality to heterosexuality, that efforts to change are not generally harmful....
>
> Those who have received help from reorientation therapists have collectively stood up to be counted – as once did their openly gay counterparts in the 1970s. On May 22, 1994, in Philadelphia, the American Psychiatric Association was protested against for the first time in history – not by pro-gay activists, but by a group of people reporting that they had substantially changed their sexual orientation and that change is possible for others (Davis, 1994). The same thing happened at the 2000 Psychiatric Association convention in Chicago (Gorner, 2000), and again at the 2006 APA convention in New Orleans (Foust, 2006).
>
> The APA cannot ethically deny treatment for unwanted homosexuality as long as there are patients who seek it and therapists who are competent and willing to provide this service after offering proper informed consent procedures. It would contradict the APA's own code of ethics to deny such treatment. The APA states, "Mental health organizations call on their members to respect a person's [client's] right to self-determination" (2008, p. 3). By the same token, a client who is not distressed about his sexual orientation should not be directed to change, and therapy affirming homosexuality should be available for any client who seeks it. Client self-determination is one of the cornerstones of any form of psychological care.[126]

For LGBTQ people who want change in their sexual preferences, there is genuine hope for change. Dr. Foster and his colleges at Pure Passion have already videoed several hundred testimonies of such in several languages.[127] It is clearly false to believe that some people are born gay and so they cannot change, or that science has shown that belief to be true.

We've already seen that New Zealand government scientific researcher Neil Whitehead writes, "About half of the homosexual/bisexual population (in a non-therapeutic environment) moves towards heterosexuality over a lifetime. About 3 percent of the present heterosexual population once firmly believed themselves to be homosexual or bisexual. Sexual orientation is not set in concrete."[128] Don't expect that to be reported in secular school "comprehensive" sex ed courses.

From Brook,

Why do some countries and some churches not let gays get married? Is this fair?

From Ms. Barb,

Remember that Jesus said, "This explains why a man leaves his father and mother and is joined to his wife, and the two are united into one" (Matthew 19:5). Here He's talking about Genesis 1:28 when God created Adam and Eve and told them, "Be fruitful and multiply. Fill the earth and govern it." Every country and church in our world lets their adults do that, provided that the husband and wife are not close relatives. Even people who call themselves gay share the same privileges to marry a spouse of the opposite sex, and many have done so. But in the 21st century some gays have demanded that all countries and churches also let them marry their favourite same-sex partner.[129] That demand misunderstands what marriage is.

The video *Made for Each Other: Sexual difference is essential to marriage* shows what marriage actually is. The video description says,

> ... Josh and Carrie talk about why men and women matter for marriage. Their dialogue and interactions illuminate the beauty of sexual difference and complementarity between man and woman as husband and wife. Only

> through sexual difference can a husband and a wife give themselves completely to one another – so completely that "the two become one flesh" (Gen 2:24). True marital union is not possible without sexual difference.... Protecting and promoting marriage as the union of one man and one woman isn't arbitrary or discriminatory. Rather, it's a matter of justice, truth, love, and real freedom. Only a man and a woman – at every level of their identity: biological, physiological, emotional, social, spiritual – are capable of authentically speaking the language of married love, that is, the language of total self-gift, open to the gift of the other and the gift of life.[130]

Countries and churches that "marry" two men who are having sex or two women who are having sex are changing *marriage* from what God designed it to be into a contract between two adult sex partners who can never enjoy sex as God designed it to be or produce children with a real mom and dad. Sure, same-sex couples may have brought children into their relationship through previous sexual relationships. They may even produce new children with the help of others. And kids who follow Christ should never tease or shame either those kids or their parents. All humans are worthy of our *agape*-love and respect, no matter what they believe or do. That does not mean that what they believe or do is right. Kids who follow Christ understand that.

But true *marriage* is not merely about uniting two people who deeply love each other. Governments are not concerned about people's romantic relationships. But governments are concerned about social stability and the care of children. True marriage *unites* a man and a woman *exclusively for life. It provides a mom and dad to kids who are born to them or adopted by them.* It prevents uniting three or more people who deeply love each other.[131] Kids who follow Christ understand that.

Sure, some families break up (for example, through death,

divorce, or abandonment), so some kids can't grow up with their biological mom and dad. Sure, some moms heroically raise their kids without their biological dad, and some dads heroically raise their kids without their biological mom, but *no mom can actually be a dad to her kids* and *no dad can actually be a mom to his kids.* "What we know from the social sciences is that biology matters, gender matters and stability matters."[132] Also some divorcees, widows, and widowers remarry. Their kids then get a step-mom or a step-dad. Some kids grow up with a mom who never married or with grandparents or other relatives. Some kids get adopted and can have a great life with their adoptive parents. That all helps, but it's not the same as growing up with their biological *mom and dad.* We live in a messed-up world. Kids who follow Christ understand that. How about childless couples? Ryan Anderson notes, "Not every marriage will have a child, but every child has a mother and a father, and marriage exists to unite that mother and father with the child."[133]

From Brook,

My friend says that anyone who thinks that LGBTQ sex is wrong might be a dangerous "extremist." What can I say about this?

From Ms. Barb,

There are some leaders, in some countries, who classify certain speech as hate speech and have put in place laws to punish those who speak such. Christians who speak against the sinful practices of LGBTQ are wrongly placed in this category. So, your friend is right if he or she might be thinking

AT OUR HOUSE

1. **Ask your parents what they think of what the Bible says about gay sex, Christian gays, and why.**
2. **Ask your parents how they respond to "gay marriage."**
3. **Ask your parents whether they think people can change sexual preferences.**

of the prime minister of Britain saying that Britain cannot "tolerate intolerance," or Britain's education secretary saying that comments by children that they consider homosexuality to be "wrong" or "evil" could "trigger" concerns from teachers under guidance designed to help schools detect possible radicalization.[134] We need to understand that the British laws referred to were an effort to stop religious violence, and in their zeal to do so, they may include Bible-believing Christians by accident. In such a situation it may be helpful to say that schools are places where many ideas can be safely explored, that as a Bible-believing Christian you agree that homosexual practices are "wrong" or "evil" but that you also love and respect the people who do them because they too are created in God's image.

The apostle John adds a simple warning: So don't be surprised, dear brothers and sisters, if the world hates you (1 John 3:13). Be especially careful of slick slogans like "Love is love," "Hatred is not a family value," or "Celebrate diversity" (in rainbow colours).[135] They are often used in "bumper sticker ethics." Politicians and educators argue that we should all be free to be who we are and to love who we love. That sounds right, but does this mean that pedophiles (adults who like to have sex with kids) should be free to be pedophiles and polyamorous people (two or more women married to two or more men) should be free to be polyamorous? We are all free to be sinners. That does not mean we actually are free to go on sinning without consequences. We are all free to love who we love, particularly if we *agape*-love everyone as created in God's image. That does not mean we actually are free to have sex with everyone and anyone, without consequences in this life or the next. God's design for sex is that it be enjoyed within a sacred marriage covenant as God ordained between one husband and one wife. Kids who follow Christ learn to *agape*-love everyone as created in God's image, and, where appropriate, to show that love by warning others of the dangers of their sexual misbehaviour. Such warnings must be clearly expressions of *agape*-love, never of hate or anger. Former lesbian activist and university professor of English and women's studies, Dr. Rosaria Butterfield, warns that "homosexuality is not a behavior to be modified [changed], it's a sin to be mortified [put to death]."[136]

In Romans 12:1–2 Paul writes,

> And so, dear brothers and sisters, I plead with you to give your bodies to God because of all he has done for you. Let them be a living and holy sacrifice – the kind he will find acceptable. This is truly the way to worship him. Don't copy the behavior and customs of this world, but let God transform you into a new person by changing the way you think. Then you will learn to know God's will for you, which is good and pleasing and perfect.

Sadly in our world today, many non-Christian people (and even some who call themselves Christians) really believe that many beliefs and behaviours that the Bible teaches as true and right are actually false and wrong. For example, many believe that it is actually false and wrong to believe that God created Adam and Eve in His likeness and blessed them with sex organs beautifully designed for sexual intercourse only with each other as a married couple in a lifelong covenant marriage, for their joy, pleasure, and to pro-create kids whom they were to raise to be whole as God intended.

12 TRUTH, GRACE, AND FORGIVENESS IN A MESSED-UP WORLD

Our world is a mess, mainly because people are a mess. Of course, people disagree about what is good, just, and true. We have disagreed ever since the serpent convinced Eve in the Garden of Eden that God was mean (not loving), that she and Adam would enjoy a fuller life if they disobeyed God by eating the forbidden fruit. She and Adam fell for that lie, and everyone ever since has also messed up. That's why it's sometimes so hard to grow up in Christ. But God sent Christ to die in our place to pay for our sin guilt and to tell us the truth about us, God, and all we need to know to grow up in Christ. Still Satan and his hosts keep lying to everyone, in a battle to mess up everyone in his war against God and what is good, just, and true.

Paul writes in Ephesians 6,

> A final word: *Be strong in the Lord and in his mighty power.* Put on all of God's armor so that you will be able to *stand firm* against all strategies of the devil. For we are not fighting against flesh-and-blood enemies, but against evil rulers and authorities of the unseen world, against mighty powers in this dark world, and against evil spirits in the heavenly places. (Emphasis added.)

This is serious business. But this need not scare any Christian kid who really wants to grow up in Christ. Paul also writes in 1 Corinthians 15:57–58, But thank God! *He gives us victory over* sin and death through our Lord Jesus Christ. So, my dear brothers and sisters, *be strong and immovable. Always work enthusiastically for the Lord,* for you know that nothing you do for the Lord is ever useless. (Emphasis added.)

Paul also writes in 2 Corinthians 10:3–5,

> We are human, but we don't wage war as humans do. *We use God's mighty weapons,* not worldly weapons, to knock down the strongholds of human reasoning and to *destroy false arguments*. We destroy every proud obstacle that keeps people from knowing God. We capture their rebellious thoughts and *teach them to obey Christ.* (Emphasis added.)

We need to lean heavily on the supernatural power of the Holy Spirit as we seek what is actually good, just, and true, because we know that the war over these issues is waged against an invisible demonic enemy who loves to mess up, not only the world, but also as many Christians as he can.

Note how the apostle John counsels believers in 1 John 2:15–29:

> *Do not love this world nor the things it offers* you, for when you love the world, you do not have the love of the Father in you. For the *world offers only a craving for physical pleasure,* a craving for everything we see, and *pride* in our achievements and *possessions*. These are *not from the Father*, but are from this world. And *this world is fading away*, along with everything that people crave. But *anyone who does what pleases God will live forever.*
>
> Dear children, the last hour is here. You have heard that the Antichrist is coming, and already many such antichrists have appeared. From this we know that the last hour has come. These *people left our churches, but they never really belonged with us*; otherwise they would have stayed with us. When they left, it proved that they did not belong with us.
>
> But you are not like that, for the *Holy One has given you his Spirit, and all of you know the truth.* So I am writing to you not because you don't know the truth but because *you know the difference between truth and lies*. And who is a liar? Anyone who says that Jesus is not the Christ. Anyone who denies the Father and the Son is an antichrist. Anyone who denies the Son doesn't have the Father, either. But anyone who acknowledges the Son

AT OUR HOUSE

1. **Discuss 1 John 2: 15–29 with your parents.**
2. **Ask your parents how they respond to those who reject Christ.**

> has the Father also.
>
> So *you must remain faithful* to what you have been taught from the beginning. If you do, you will remain in fellowship with the Son and with the Father. And in this fellowship we *enjoy the eternal life* he promised us.
>
> I am writing these things to *warn you about those who want to lead you astray.* But you have received the *Holy Spirit*, and he lives within you, so you don't need anyone to teach you what is true. For the Spirit teaches you everything you need to know, and *what he teaches is true – it is not a lie.* So just as he has taught you, remain in fellowship with Christ.
>
> And now, dear children, *remain in fellowship with Christ so that when he returns, you will be full of courage* and not shrink back from him in shame.
>
> Since we know that *Christ is righteous,* we also know that *all who do what is right are God's children.* (Emphasis added.)

Notice that "the world" that John here tells us not to love, is the world of Christ-rejecting false beliefs. That's different from the world of people that God loves (John 3:16) and so should we.

In his gospel (John 16:1–4, 7–9, 13–14) the apostle John also told us what Jesus said to His disciples before He went to the cross to die for us:

> "I have told you these things *so that you won't abandon your faith.* For you will be expelled from the synagogues, and the time is coming when those who kill you will think they are doing a holy service for God. This is because they have never known the Father or me. Yes, I'm telling you these things now, so that when they happen, you will remember my warning....
>
> But in fact, it is best for you that I go away, because if I don't, the *Advocate* won't come. If I do go away, then I will send him to you. And when he comes, *he will convict the world of its sin, and of God's righteousness, and of the coming judgment. The world's sin is that it refuses to believe in me....*
>
> When the *Spirit of truth* comes, he will guide you into all truth. He will not speak on his own but will tell you what he has heard. He will tell you about the future. *He will bring me glory* by telling you

AT OUR HOUSE

1. **Discuss how the Holy Spirit works today.**
2. **Ask your parents how they decide what is true, just and good.**

> whatever he receives from me." (Emphasis added.)

Kids who follow Christ need the Holy Spirit, the "Spirit of truth," to bring glory to Christ and protect them from the world's lies.

From Ryan,

What is "truth"?

From Uncle Al,

Good question, Ryan. This is often called "Pilate's question" (John 18:38). Though most people agree that bullying must be stopped, there are major disagreements over sex, marriage, pornography, abortion, and so on. On both sides of such issues, enthusiasts often disagree over what "truth" is,[137] what the relevant "facts" are, what those facts mean, and how they should be shared with others. Too often these debates deteriorate to anger, hate, lying, accusations of lying, law suits, and insults. Such behaviours are never okay for kids who really want to grow up in Christ. God created everyone in His image. That means we should treat everyone with *agape*-love and respect. That's what "grace" means. Does that mean we should agree with all their beliefs and behaviours? Of course not.

Paul warns us in 1 Timothy 4:1–3,

> Now the Holy Spirit tells us clearly that in the *last times some will turn away from the true faith*; they will follow deceptive spirits and teachings that come from demons. These people are hypocrites and liars, and their consciences are dead.
>
> They will say it is wrong to be married and wrong to eat certain foods. But God created those foods to be eaten with thanks by *faithful people who know the truth.* (Emphasis added.)

Kids who really want to grow up in Christ will always want to be among the "faithful people who know the truth" and who also live it and speak it with *agape*-love and grace to those who reject it as false.

Take, for example, the debate over the fashionable belief that gays are born that way and can never change. This was first argued by Hungarian journalist Karl-Maria Kertbeny in 1869. Lots of LGBTQ studies since then have tried to prove it is true. They have all failed. Lots of scholars, journalists, governments, judges, laws, professional societies, and others have believed that it is true. But lots of ex-gays have reported that, in their cases at least, it is false. Some ex-gays left that behaviour pattern on their own; some were helped by counsellors, either secular or religious (for example, Muslim, Jewish, Christian, Mormon). Some ex-gays left that behaviour pattern suddenly, some slowly. Some ex-gays report that they once believed they were born that way and can never change; some never did believe it. Some ex-gays report they continue to struggle sometimes with same-sex attractions (SSA); some don't. (The same happens for ex-alcoholics and ex-smokers.) Some ex-gays marry and raise families, some don't. Some ex-gays return to their old gay behaviour pattern, most don't. Some ex-gays stay single and celibate (that is, they abstain from sex acts of all kinds all their remaining lives). Some OT prophets stayed single and celibate as did Jesus and Paul – nothing wrong with that.

Except in cases of rape, virtually every time person A has an actual sexual experience with person B (not mere fantasy) both have made a choice about that, regardless of what their habitual preferences or tendencies might be at the time. Those choices make lasting impressions. (Remember, neuroplasticity of the brain?) If they then say "I'm gay and I can't change," they may really believe that, even if it is a lie. Kids who follow Christ treat such people with graceful compassion and respect, even if these kids are convinced that the gays have rejected the truth about themselves.

Take, for another example, the debate over a woman's "right" to choose abortion, if she decides not to have a baby at the time she gets pregnant. Some even refuse to use the word "abortion." Instead they just talk of "terminating a pregnancy" – same thing. Think back to how your life began. About nine months before you were born, Brook and Ryan, your dad's sperm fertilized your mom's ovum and a new cell was formed with DNA different from your mom's and your dad's. Brook, that cell and every one of the 37 trillion cells in your body ever since has had XX chromosomes delivered by your dad's sperm, and Ryan, that cell and every cell in your body ever since has had XY chromosomes. Notice how every cell in your body shows whether you are a boy or a girl, no matter how you feel, or what drugs or surgery you might have done.

Besides truth, kids who want to grow up in Christ need to understand and practise God's grace. In his comments on Jesus coming to earth, John writes (John 1:14 NIV) The Word became flesh and made his dwelling among us. We have seen his glory, the glory of the one and only Son, who came from the Father, full of *grace and truth.*" (Emphasis added.)

Paul writes in Titus 2:8,11–15

> *Teach the truth* so that your teaching can't be criticized. Then those who oppose us will be ashamed and have nothing bad to say about us....
>
> For the *grace of God has been revealed*, bringing salvation to all people. And we are instructed to *turn from godless living and sinful pleasures.* We should *live in this evil world with wisdom, righteousness, and devotion to God*, while we look forward with *hope* to that wonderful day when the glory of our great God and Savior, Jesus Christ, will be revealed. He gave his life to free us from every kind of sin, to cleanse us, and to *make us his very own people, totally committed to doing good deeds.*
>
> You must *teach these things and encourage the believers to do them.* You have the *authority to correct* them when necessary, so don't let anyone disregard what you say. (Emphasis added.)

From Ryan,

How can I help my friend who thinks he is gay?

From Uncle Al,

Good question, Ryan. Our world is a mess, mainly because people are a mess. That includes every one of us, not just those who think they might be gay. That means we all need forgiveness. So does everyone else. Each of us makes mistakes. Each of us sins. When we or someone else sins, the first step is to pray for special Holy Spirit power to deal in *agape*-love, truth, and holiness with the whole situation in a God-glorifying way. That should help us avoid all bullying, name-calling, and shaming.

Next notice 1 John 1:8–2:2:

> *If we claim we have no sin, we are only fooling ourselves and not living in the truth. But if we confess our sins to him, he is faithful and just to forgive us our sins and to cleanse us from all wickedness.* If we claim we have not sinned, we are calling God a liar and showing that his word has no place in our hearts....
>
> My dear children, I am writing this to you *so that you will not sin. But if anyone does sin, we have an advocate who pleads our case before the Father. He is Jesus Christ, the one who is truly righteous. He himself is the sacrifice that atones for our sins* – and not only our sins but the sins of all the world. (Emphasis added.)

Notice that it is not sin to be tempted, as Jesus was. Hebrews 4:15 reads This High Priest of ours understands our weaknesses, for he faced all of the same testings we do, yet he did not sin.

So, Ryan, even if your friend struggles with same-sex attractions (SSA) that's not sin so long as he disciplines himself to avoid fantasizing about doing same-sex acts or actually doing them. Likely we all are tempted to lie or steal sometimes, or even to have sex outside marriage. It's only when we fantasize about doing such sins or yield to the temptation and actually do them that we actually sin. That's when we need to "confess" (agree with God about what we did and that it's wrong). We need to "repent" (turn away from the sin and toward Christ our Lord – Mark 6:12).

Notice also that our temptations need not define who we "are." Though some drivers habitually drive over the speed limit, their speeding need not define who they are. Similarly our favourite sins need not define who we are. In that sense we can say that we all are sinners for whom Christ died, but no one really "is" gay. Even those people who like to have gay sex are really "sinners for whom Christ died" just like the rest of us, but they are not "gay people," even if they define who they are that way. Such identities merely reinforce the 1869 journalist's myth that some people are born that way and can never change. Don't expect to learn this in secular "comprehensive" sex ed anywhere.

In Luke 9:23 Jesus said to the crowd, "If any of you wants to be my follower, you must turn from your selfish ways, take up your cross daily, and follow me." For anyone who wants to grow up in Christ, that's a great identity: simply view yourself as a follower of Jesus.[138] That includes daily dying to our selfish ways.[139]

Ryan, suggest that your friend seek sound professional Christian help with his SSA. One good way is to visit Restored Hope Network at http://www.restoredhopenetwork.org/. Also, urge your friend to see the full video, *Such Were Some of You* at http://suchweresomeofyou.org/.

> [It] confronts the rising tide of popular opinion by chronicling the stories of 29 former homosexual men and women who say that Jesus Christ has transformed their lives. Experts in psychology (Dr. Julie Hamilton), biblical scholarship (Dr. Robert Gagnon) and ministry (Dr. Neil Anderson) add their voice to the claim that people have been leaving homosexuality for millennia.[140]

Also share with your friend the many serious health risks that regularly go with the gay lifestyle already discussed in Chapter 10. As a true friend, speak the truth in love (Ephesians 4:15). All sin is an expression of our rebellion against God (Rom. 1:19–32).

From Brook,

My friend got pregnant and had an abortion. Now she wonders if she made the right choice. What can I do to help her?

AT OUR HOUSE

1. **Discuss what you or your parents should do if a friend got pregnant when they are not ready for a baby.**

Bonus: Visit a near-by crisis pregnancy centre.

From Ms. Barb,

Good question, Brook. The decision to abort an unborn child is often complicated by the advice of many others with an interest in that decision. Often those others fail to understand the sense of grief over the loss of the son or daughter that the mother may not have loved enough to save. Some mothers hardly sense that grief at all. Others carry it much of the rest of their lives. In either case, usually life goes on, except for those who end their lives in despair. Your friend most urgently needs to receive the forgiveness that comes only from repentance and faith in Christ's atoning sacrifice. It may be that the best way to help your friend is to show her much *agape*-love in her time of doubt, remorse, and grief.

Perhaps in the process she may tell you that she was raped or otherwise sexually abused. In that case, she is a victim of crime and this should be reported to police. She'll need a friend to walk with her in this troubling process. Perhaps she'll invite you to be that friend. Part of showing *agape*-love is to show you care deeply but won't ask prying questions. Let her talk when she is ready and make sure you listen carefully without trying to fix everything right away. Perhaps she'll need help from her parents and her pastor.

Perhaps you might invite your friend to read with you a *Christian Post* article about the "True Love Waits" project. It reads in part,

> "The project will have a greater focus on God's grace and mercy for those of us who have been abused, who have made mistakes in relationships, or who have guilt and shame resulting from sexual sin," said King. "I want people to know that God doesn't hate them because of their past, but that in Jesus Christ they can be forgiven, healed, and redeemed. Just because they messed up, it doesn't mean they give up."... "If Jesus is your Lord, then you will gladly do what He says, trusting that because He loves you and He knows what's best for you," said King to CP... "His standards of abstinence before marriage and fidelity within marriage are for your own joy and happiness. Submitting yourself to the Lordship of Christ in the area of your sexuality is also a witness to the world that you belong to Jesus." ... "The good news is that

> temptation, lust, porn, sex, shame, and guilt are no match for the grace that Jesus offers us. If True Love Project gives people a better view of the beauty and majesty of Jesus Christ, if it inspires them to bring their past mistakes and failures to Jesus, if it helps them receive His forgiveness and move past the shame of their sin, if it helps them set standards for what is right and wrong in dating relationships, and if it helps them see love as serving and sacrificing, then it will leave a legacy that I would be proud of," said King. [141]

Learning a habit of forgiveness is a major success factor in growing up in Christ. When someone does you wrong, it's natural to feel irritated. But you can control your temper, not get angry or bitter, or seek revenge or hold a grudge. In Leviticus 19:18 God says, "Do not seek revenge or bear a grudge against a fellow Israelite, but love your neighbor as yourself. I am the LORD."

In Romans 12:9–21 Paul writes,

> Don't just pretend to love others. *Really love them. Hate what is wrong.* Hold tightly to what is good. Love each other with genuine affection, and take delight in honoring each other. Never be lazy, but work hard and serve the Lord enthusiastically. Rejoice in our confident hope. *Be patient in trouble, and keep on praying.* When God's people are in need, be ready to help them. Always be eager to practice hospitality.
>
> *Bless those who persecute you. Don't curse them; pray that God will bless them.* Be happy with those who are happy, and weep with those who weep. *Live in harmony with each other.* Don't be too proud to enjoy the company of ordinary people. And *don't think you know it all!*
>
> Never pay back evil with more evil. Do things in such a way that everyone can see you are honorable. *Do all that you can to live in peace with everyone.*
>
> Dear friends, *never take revenge*. Leave that to the righteous anger of God. For the Scriptures say, "I will take revenge; I will pay them back," says the LORD.
>
> Instead, "If your enemies are hungry, feed them. If they are thirsty, give them something to drink. In doing this, you will heap burning coals of shame on their heads."
>
> Don't let evil conquer you, but *conquer evil by doing good.* (Emphasis added.)

A particularly challenging situation is when someone accuses you of doing wrong, but you are really convinced that you are innocent of the charge. This will test your skills at active listening to hear out your accuser's understanding of what actually happened and why it happened. Be as compassionately open as you can to the possibility that your accuser is really right, and that you really did wrong. If so, be quick to apologize and ask for forgiveness. If you cannot honestly agree about what happened and why, or about whether what you did or said was wrong, you might suggest that you both ask someone more mature to hear both of your stories and recommend a way to settle your differences without sin. Jesus taught, In Matthew 18:15–17,

> "If another believer sins against you, *go* privately and point out the offense. If the other person listens and confesses it, you have won that person back. But *if you are unsuccessful, take one or two others with you and go back again,* so that everything you say may be confirmed by two or three witnesses. If the person still refuses to listen, *take your case to the church.* Then if he or she won't accept the church's decision, treat that person as a pagan or a corrupt tax collector. (Emphasis added.)

Likely in most cases "take your case to the church" refers only to rather serious disagreements, and only to church leaders, not the whole church. Likely Jesus' teaching to treat anyone as "a pagan or a corrupt tax

AT OUR HOUSE

1. **Discuss the best ways to be a true friend to someone who identifies as "gay."**
2. **Discuss the best way to forgive someone who has really wronged you.**
3. **Discuss the best way to deal with someone who thinks you have wronged them, but you believe you are innocent of the charge.**
4. **Do a Bible study with your parents on Romans 12.**

Bonus: Visit a pastor or youth leader to hear their views on #1–3 above.

collector" means that we not exclude this person from our love, but that we show them love by praying for them and sharing Jesus' gospel with them.

In our culture it has become popular for "pro-choice" advocates to accuse "pro-life" advocates of hating women. Similarly, if you believe that same-sex sex is wrong, and are convinced that you really love people who disagree with you, then you can expect to be called a hater. When you face such false accusations, remember Paul's instructions in Ephesians 4:31, Get rid of all bitterness, rage, anger, harsh words, and slander, as well as all types of evil behavior. You might ask your accuser, "Are you a tolerant person?" Usually people will claim that they are tolerant people. Then challenge them to tolerate you, even if you disagree with them on any issue. Rick Warren observes,

> Our culture has accepted two huge lies. The first is that if you disagree with someone's lifestyle, you must fear or hate them. The second is that to love someone means you agree with everything they believe or do. Both are nonsense. You don't have to compromise convictions to be compassionate.[142]

Kids who grow up in Christ faithfully learn the truth of God, His grace and forgiveness and how to show this to others.

13 NETWORK WITH OTHER FOLLOWERS OF CHRIST

Our world is a mess. We are known by the company we keep and the choices we make. ("Birds of a feather flock together.") Likely you've already made some good friends. Likely you're already regular in some Bible-believing Sunday school, perhaps also an evening club, sports team, or other networking group with other kids who want to grow up in Christ. If not, you may seek out such settings where you can enjoy great fun and learn to serve others in the name of Jesus.

Next to your parents, a network of good Christian friends may be the most important part in your growing up in Christ. To become a whole follower of Christ you will want to set God-glorifying goals, choose a Christ-honouring career, develop devotional habits that strengthen your prayer life and your understanding of the Bible and how it speaks to the culture of our times. If you can find friends who encourage you in all these areas, you will be doubly blessed. That's part of why it is so important to get regularly involved in some Bible-believing youth group, perhaps a camp, some mission outreach ministries, or other networking group of like-minded kids.

Remember that all these other people are sinners too, that some conflicts are sure to happen, and that you need to learn patience, grace, kindness, and forgiveness to deal with conflicts. Such experiences may develop your leadership gifts and other talents in music, counselling, witnessing to God's truth, and so on. Jesus' disciples were very imperfect people. But He trusted them as His friends (John 15:15) to turn the world upside down after He was gone back to heaven.

In 1 Samuel 20 we read of the wonderful friendship between young David and Jonathan, son of wicked King Saul. Verse 17 reads, And Jonathan made David reaffirm his vow of friendship again, for Jonathan loved David as he loved himself. Not every tween who desires such a close friend really wants to grow up in Christ. Those that do, are doubly blessed.

On the other hand, James warns us not to get too close a friendship with the world. In James 4:4 he writes, Don't you realize that friendship with the world makes you an enemy of God? I say it again: If you want to be a friend of the world, you make yourself an enemy of God. Followers of Christ can and should *agape*-love and respect all unbelievers without becoming their very best friends so as to learn to think, talk, and behave like them. In 1 Corinthians 15:33 Paul warns, Don't be fooled by those who say such things, for "bad company corrupts good character." The first Psalm begins with, Oh, the joys of those who do not follow the advice of the wicked, or stand around with sinners, or join in with mockers. But they delight in the law of the LORD, meditating on it day and night.

You likely will have some doubts along the way, especially when you dialogue with others in high school, university, and elsewhere who reject God and the Bible as myths, or who insist that to have fun you need to sin in various ways. Books 4 and 5 in this series are designed to help you navigate many of these turbulent waters safely so that you can grow up strong in Christ and learn the real joys of abiding in Him. Choose your friends carefully, even among born-again Christians. Choose wise followers of Jesus as your best friends. Weed out the ones who tend to lead you astray. You and your friends will learn much from each other. Make sure that what you all learn from each other helps you all grow up in Christ better. The number of your friends does not matter. Their spiritual quality as followers of Jesus matters a great deal. For example, are they conformed to this world's values, or are they transformed by God's Word and His Holy

14 GROW UP AS FOLLOWERS OF CHRIST

Your tween years (8 to 12) and teen years (13 to 19) will likely be the time of your life when you will decide most clearly whether you will be a "fan" of Jesus or a follower of Jesus. (See the description of "fan" further on.) You will likely make many commitments and form many habits that will shape most profoundly whether you grow up in Christ, and if so, how you grow up in Christ.

In Matthew 22:37 Jesus quoted Deuteronomy 6:5, Jesus replied, "**You must love the Lord your God with all your heart, all your soul, and all your mind.**" Followers of Jesus are totally in love with Him. Loving anyone or anything else more than God is idolatry. The Lord our God is the only One who truly completes us. He's the only One worthy of our total devotion, our ultimate love with all our heart, soul, and mind. Yes, we love others around the world (even those who prefer to see themselves as our enemies) as God does, with self-sacrificing *agape*-love. Yes, we love our friends with *phileo*-love and our family with *storge*-love. And there may come a time when you are grown up that you will fall in *eros*-love and get married. But to become a real follower of Jesus your ultimate love with all your heart, soul and mind needs to be for the Lord your God.

In John 6 we read several very encouraging stories in Jesus' ministry. In verses 1–15 Jesus fed a huge crowd of over 5,000. In verses 16–21 the disciples are at sea in a terrible storm when they see Jesus walking on the water. Next day that crowd asked to be fed again, but Jesus told them that He was the "bread of life," through whom they could have eternal life. Then a shocker in verse 66: At this point many of his disciples turned away and deserted him. Why? Kyle Idleman, in *Not a Fan: Becoming a Completely Committed Follower of Jesus*, argues that the crowd that wanted to be fed were just "fans," like sports fans that just show up for their favourite team's games. They leave after the game. They are not really committed followers. Idleman writes,

> Fans don't mind him doing a little touch-up work, but Jesus wants complete renovation. Fans come to Jesus thinking tune-up, but Jesus is thinking overhaul. Fans think a little makeup is fine, but Jesus is thinking makeover. Fans think a little decorating is required, but Jesus wants a complete remodel. Fans want Jesus to inspire them, but Jesus wants to interfere with their lives.[143]

In fact Jesus said some things that turn fans away from actually following Him. In Luke 9:23 we read, Then he said to the crowd, "If any of you wants to be my follower, you must give up your own way, take up your cross daily, and follow me." In Matthew 10:38 Jesus said: "If you refuse to take up your cross and follow me, you are not worthy of being mine." Actually following Jesus means being so in love with Him that our choices and characters reflect His.

Jesus did a lot of praying, and so should we, if we really want to follow Him.[144] A good place to start is with the prayer Jesus taught His disciples in His Sermon on the Mount (Matt. 6:9–13):

> Pray like this: Our Father in heaven, may your name be kept holy. May your Kingdom come soon. May your will be done on earth, as it is in heaven. Give us today the food we need, and forgive us our sins, as we have forgiven those who sin against us. And don't let us yield to temptation, but rescue us from the evil one. [Some texts add: For yours is the kingdom and the power and the glory forever. Amen.]

Another helpful guide to prayer is the ACTS outline: Adoration, Confession, Thanksgiving and Supplication. Check out the good videos on this subject available on YouTube.[145]

Jesus' life and work were saturated by God's Word, and so should ours, if we really want to follow Him.[146] Youth pastor David Winston gives five reasons young Christians should read the Bible: 1) reading the Bible transforms our thinking; 2) Bible reading helps us hear God's voice; 3) God's Word is our instructional manual for life; 4) by reading God's Word we are sowing the Word seed in our heart; 5) reading the Bible helps to transform our self-image into the image of Christ.[147]

Learning to grow your love for Jesus through a growing life of prayer and Bible study can be an exciting adventure. Regular active participation in the life of a strong Bible-believing church can add richly to that adventure. Christ established strong churches as a community of friends growing in Christ. Find one that is this and help your friends there grow in Christ.

May God guide and bless you with His best for you as you grow up in Christ. Our prayers continue with you in this most fulfilling life pursuit!

GLOSSARY/ WORDS to KNOW[148]

This is a selection of terms some may find suitable for tweens. Pronunciation is included in parentheses, with accented syllables printed in all capitals. Underlined words are defined elsewhere in this glossary.

Abstinence (AHB-stin-ens): the practice of not doing something, e.g., drinking alcohol or having sex.

Acne (AK-nee): the normal, temporary, but often frustrating, skin condition of puberty, when the skin's oil glands make too much oil and skin pores get stopped up with oil, dead skin, and bacteria, forming pimples. Then the skin around these clogged pores can swell and look lumpy or red.

Anus (AY-nus): the opening where bowel movements (also known as "poop" or "stool") come out. In other words, it's the hole in the bottom of your digestive system.

Anal sex (anal intercourse): sexual activity that involves inserting a male penis into the anus of a male or female.

Bladder (BLAH-der): the bag where your body collects liquid wastes.

Bowel movement (BM)**:** the action of "pooping" or "passing your stool" or "going to the bathroom" to get rid of your body's solid wastes; most people don't like to talk about this.

Cervix (SERV-ix): the lower part of a female uterus.

Clitoris (KLIT-or-is): a small, sensitive protrusion just inside the inner (minor) labia where the two folds meet on top; it is very sensitive to sexual arousal and can become erect if stimulated.

Conceive (con-SEEV): (verb) the event in which a male sperm fertilizes a female ovum, which then implants in the wall of the mother's uterus so that a baby begins to grow.

Conception (con-SEP-shun): (noun) the moment when a male sperm fertilizes a female ovum, which then implants in the wall of the mother's uterus so that a baby begins to grow

Condom (CON-dohm): a rubbery contraceptive device to prevent fluids from moving from one sex partner to another.

Contraceptive (CON-trah-SEP-tiv): any device or method to prevent the female sex partner from getting pregnant as a result of sexual intercourse.

Ejaculate (eeh-JAK-yoo-laht): (verb) to expel semen from the penis.

Estrogen (EST-row-jen): a female hormone that controls the development of young girls into women who can bear and nurse babies.

Fertilize (FER-til-iz): (verb) the event when a male sperm enters a female ovum so that a baby is conceived.

Foreskin (FOR-skin): the loose skin that covers the male penis shaft and glans; if the man is circumcised the glans may not be covered.

Genitals (JEN-i-tahlz): the reproductive organs in males and females, especially the external reproductive organs.

Glans (GLANZ): an enlarged bulbous-shaped tip of the penis.

Fallopian tubes (fuh-LO-pee-un): the tubes that carry an ovum (egg cell) from the ovary to the uterus once a month.

Hormones (HOR-mohnz): chemicals that your pituitary gland makes to help the body do certain things – like grow up!

Labia (LEH-bee-ah): larger outer (major) lips and smaller inner (minor) lips that protect a female's clitoris, vagina and urethra openings. During puberty, pubic hair begins to grow on the labia major.

Menopause (MEHN-oh-pawz): the transition when middle-aged women stop ovulating and menstruating.

Menstrual flow (also called menstruation, menses, or period) (MEN-strul): the process and time that any unfertilized ovum and the blood lining of the uterus are shed to begin a woman's new cycle.

Monogamous relationship (moh-NOG-om-us): a relationship in which two people (normally a husband and wife) agree to have sex with no one else but each other, and both stick to that agreement.

Neuroplasticity (NEW-roh-plas-TI-ci-tee): aspects of the brain continue to change (or are "plastic") even into adulthood.

Oral sex (OR-al): sexual activity that involves any contact between one partner's mouth and another partner's genitals.

Ovaries (OHV-ah-reez): small, oval-shaped glands located on either side of the uterus that produce eggs (ova) and hormones.

Ovulation (OWHV-yoo-lah-shun): the process and time of a woman's ovum moving from an ovary to a fallopian tube on the way to the uterus.

Ovum (OH-vum): the woman's egg cell that may be fertilized by a man's sperm to begin a baby's growth.

Penis (PEE-nis): the main external male organ used in urination and for penetrating the female vagina in sexual intercourse.

Pituitary gland (pih-TOO-uh-ter-ee): a pea-shaped gland located at the bottom of the brain that releases special hormones to start puberty.

Pregnancy (PREG-nan-see): the process during which a woman has a baby growing in her uterus.

Prostate gland (PROHS-taht) : a male gland that controls the flow of urine during peeing and semen when a man ejaculates, but never both at the same time.

Puberty (PYOO-ber-tee): the time when the body begins to develop and change from child to adult.

Pubic hair (PYOO-bic): the hair in the frontal genital area of adolescent and adult humans, both male and female.

Scrotum (SKROT-um): a wrinkly skin bag carrying two testicles, behind a male penis.

Semen (SEE-men): a white liquid released during "wet dreams" and when a male ejaculates during sexual intercourse; it carries the sperm that might fertilize a female ovum to conceive a new baby.

Seminal vesicles (SEM-en-ahl VES-ih-kuhls): a pair of glands under the male bladder that make most of the semen.

Sexual arousal: an excitement of mind and body expecting and desiring sexual activity, especially expecting and during sexual intercourse.

Sexual intercourse (also called "making love" and several dozen other expressions): normally an erect male penis enters a female vagina, whether for pleasure or to conceive a new baby or both. Normally this bonds the partners.

Sperm (SPERM): tiny tadpole-like organisms in the semen that swim up the vagina, cervix, uterus and fallopian tubes in search of an ovum to fertilize so as to conceive a new baby.

Shaft: (SHAFT) the main part of the penis.

Stool (STUHL): solid body wastes that are passed into a toilet during a bowel movement (BM).

Testosterone (tes-TOS-ter-ohn): the male hormone that starts male puberty.

Testicles (TES-tik-uhls) or **testes** (TES-tees): the two male organisms ("balls") in the male scrotum that produce about 100 million sperm per day after puberty.

Urethra (yuuh-REE-thrah): the tube in males and females that carries urine from the bladder to the outside.

Urine (YUUH-rin): the liquid body wastes that are passed into a toilet when you pee.

Uterus (womb) (YUH-ter-us) a hollow, pear-shaped organ that is home to a developing baby; it is divided into two parts: the cervix, which is the lower part that opens into the vagina, and the main body of the uterus, called the corpus, which can easily expand to hold a developing baby. A channel through the cervix allows sperm to enter and menstrual blood to exit.

Vagina (vah-JINE-ah): a canal that joins the cervix to the outside of the female body; it also is known as the birth canal.

Vas deferens (VEYS DEF-uh-renz): a male duct that carries sperm from the testes to the prostate gland, which directs it with semen to the penis when the male ejaculates.

Vulva (VUHL-vah): the exterior female genitalia where pubic hair first grows in puberty.

PARENTS' APPENDIX

The whole *Growing Up In Christ* series promotes a biblical creation-fall-redemption-consummation perspective on human development, nurturing, and decision-making as an essential foundation for becoming a complete, mature, Christ-like Christian in every dimension. The Christian parenting challenge is to craft kids' Christian characters amid the chaos of our cultures.

This Book Three in this series is intended for you parents to read first (both Mom and Dad), then for your 8- to 12-year-old kids to read on their own (or read together, if you prefer), followed by your one-on-one conversations with each of them (or together, if you prefer). Dialogue with them about what stood out for them, any questions they may have, and the "At Our House" boxes, perhaps one chapter at a time. At your discretion, as your kids progress through their tween years, you may wish to revisit some of these sections and encourage discussions of some of the "At Our House" boxes and the suggestions below. The closer your kids get to age 12, the more Scriptures you might like to explore, possibly in NLT or NIV versions. Visit some of the websites suggested in the endnotes and the resources listed below, first by yourself, then together with your kids, as further occasions for kid-parent love-bonding conversations. Caution: Don't scare your kids. God made them beautiful. Also know your kids' friends and their parents, so there is some consistency to the values they embrace.

This book deals with a wide array of issues, some of which may not be suitable for every 8- to 12-year-old tween. Depending on many unique factors, some kids under 8 will be ready to deal with some of these issues; others at 12 may not yet be ready. As a parent, you should not hesitate to regulate both the process and the language in which these issues are discussed. Some issues you might prefer not to discuss at all, were it not for our messed-up culture in our time. Most 8- to 12-year-old tweens are likely ready to deal with most or all of these issues at some time during that period. Likely the most challenging issues for many tweens, especially for the younger ones, are those in Chapters 8 to 11. No one knows your kids better than you do. No one knows better than you at what age and in what language sensitive topics (for example, sex and bullying) should be discussed with them. Your unique love, knowledge, and concern for your kids give you a priceless privilege and an awesome responsibility for their wholesome Christian nurture. You don't want to be among the 85 percent of parents who neglect sex ed with their kids.

On the other hand, note that most parents seriously underestimate how much information and curiosity kids today have picked up from our culture by the time they reach primary grades in school. Jenson and Poyner write,

> We wrote *Good Pictures Bad Pictures* as a tool to help parents to begin a dialogue about pornography before kids become interested in it and while they still see their parents as a credible source of information.... Today's Internet creates an unprecedented opportunity to view hard-core pornography. It's accessible from any Internet-enabled device, anonymous, and affordable (so much is free). And even if your child doesn't own a mobile device, he or she … very likely has friends who do.... When it comes to kids and pornography, ignorance is risk. We live in a hypersexualized culture, so raising kids with sexual integrity requires early training. Why? A child's brain is more vulnerable to porn because it is

> designed to imitate what it sees. Additionally, a child's brain has less ability to control those imitative impulses. Viewing pornography can alter the brain's neural pathways and initiate an addiction that is often harder to overcome than drugs or alcohol.[149]

You might ask, "How is our world 'messed up' today?" Brainstorming ways in which our world today is messed up will help you discover the negative influences your kids have already encountered. Try to anticipate negative influences they are likely to encounter in media, among non-Christian peers, and in secular education, especially rejections of Christian truths, experimenting with drugs and alcohol, embrace of deviant sexual behaviour as normal, immodest fashions, adulation of celebrities, embrace of a naturalistic view of reality (for example, "Matter is all there is" and "Science has destroyed faith in God and the Bible"), and so on. Secular sex education without a biblical theological context does our kids a disservice and prompts more premature mutual exploration and experimentation to the detriment of most kids. Small wonder that sexually transmitted infections (STIs) and unwanted pregnancies tripled in the first decade or two of the new secular sex education programs of the 1970s and '80s. Small wonder that EGALE's 2011 study "Every Class in Every School"[150] found that in lesbian, gay, bisexual, transgendered and queer (LGBTQ) supportive schools, some 14.1 percent of respondents self-identified as LGBTQ, whereas Statistics Canada found the LGBTQ population over 18 to be 2 percent. This study provided the "scientific" rationale for Ontario's Bill 13 (2012), Manitoba's Bill 18 (2013) and Alberta's Bill 10 (2015).

Scriptures: Genesis 3:15–4:17; 2 Corinthians 10:3–5; Ephesians 6:12–20; Hebrews 9:20–28.

The truth of the Bible is widely rejected in our messed-up world. Resources in support of this foundational belief are included in Book Four of this series and at the related website. Since Jesus trusted Scripture as God's revealed Word, should we not do the same?

Scriptures: Matthew 5:17–19; 2 Corinthians 10:3–5;

2 Timothy 3:12–17; 1 Peter 5:8–9; 2 Peter 1:16–21.

In the west, the taboo against criticism of politically correct orthodoxies regarding "progressive" sex norms parallels the blasphemy laws of Sharia law in Muslim lands.

Parents, you need to empower your kids to grow up in Christ in a messed-up world with its own set of dogmatic norms that tolerate no criticisms. Hence, your kids need their own biblical convictions of what is true and right.

Which and how many articles and videos you access and when are at your discretion. Caution: Though most of the articles and videos referenced here share the biblical perspectives of this series, a few do not.

We provide website references solely as a convenience. We do not endorse the content, policies, or products of the referenced websites. We do not control the referenced websites and are not responsible for the accuracy, legality, or content of the referenced websites, or for that of subsequent links. Referenced website content may change without notice. Hence some URLs may have changed or disappeared from the web temporarily or permanently. Our website (www.growingupinchrist.com) and its related Facebook site "Growing Up In Christ (Education)" suggest additional resources.

Suggested Additional Resources

Chapter One

Costs of Becoming a Christian – *Holiness* J. C. Ryle (1816–1900)
http://www.monergism.com/4-costs-becoming-christian
(accessed April 14, 2014). Excerpt:
J.C. Ryle writes in his classic work *Holiness* [first published in 1877] that there are four things a person must be *ready to give up* if they wish to become a Christian.
#1: Counting the Cost: *Your Self-Righteousness*
#2: Counting the Cost: *Your Sins*
#3: Counting the Cost: *Your Love of Ease*
#4: Counting the Cost: *The Favor of the World*

Summary: *Contemplating the Four Costs*

[Before going through the four points] Let there be no mistake about my meaning. I am not examining what it costs to save a Christian's soul. I know well that it costs nothing less that the blood of the Son of God to provide atonement, and to redeem man from hell. The price paid for our redemption was nothing less than the death of Jesus Christ on Calvary. The point I want to consider is another one altogether. It is what a man must be *ready to give up* if he wishes to be saved. It is the amount of sacrifice a man must submit to if he intends to serve Christ. It is in this sense that I raise the question, *"What does it cost?"* And I believe firmly it is a most important one.

What does it cost to be a true Christian?

1) It will cost him *his self-righteousness.* He must cast away all pride and high thoughts, and conceit of his own goodness. He must be content to go to heaven as a poor sinner saved only by free grace, and owing all to the merit and righteousness of another. He must be willing to give up all trust in his own morality, respectability, praying, Bible-reading, church-going, and sacrament-receiving, and trust in nothing but Jesus Christ. Let us set down this item first and foremost in our account. To be a true Christian it will cost a man his self-righteousness.

2) It will cost a man *his sins.* He must be willing to give up every habit and practice which is wrong in God's sight. He must set his face against it, quarrel with it, break off from it, fight with it, crucify it, and labor to keep it under, whatever the world around him may say or think. He must do this honestly and fairly. There must be no separate truce with any special sin which he loves. He must count all sins as

his deadly enemies, and hate every false way. Whether little or great, whether open or secret, all his sins must be thoroughly renounced. Let us set down that item second in our account. To be a Christian it will cost a man his sins.

3) It will cost a man *his love of ease.* He must take pains and trouble, if he means to run a successful race towards heaven. He must daily watch and stand his guard, like a soldier on enemy's ground. He must take heed to his behavior every hour of the day, in every company, and in every place, in public as well as in private, among strangers as well as at home. He must be careful over his time, his tongue, his temper, his thoughts, his imaginations, his motives, his conduct in every relation of life. He must be diligent about his prayers, his Bible-reading, and his use of Sundays, with all their means of grace. "This also sounds hard. There is nothing we naturally dislike so much as 'trouble' about our religion. We hate trouble. We secretly wish we could have a 'vicarious' Christianity, and could be good by proxy, and have everything done for us. Anything that requires exertion and labor is entirely against the grain of our hearts. But the soul can have 'no gains without pains.' Let us set down that item third in our account. To be a Christian it will cost a man his love of ease."

4) It will cost a man *the favor of the world.* He must be content to be thought ill of by man if he pleases God. He must count it no strange thing to be mocked, ridiculed, slandered, persecuted, and even hated. He must not be surprised to find his opinions and practices in religion despised and held up to scorn. He must submit to be thought by many a fool, an enthusiast, and a fanatic – to have his words

perverted and his actions misrepresented. In fact, he must not marvel if some call him mad. "I dare say this also sounds hard. We naturally dislike unjust dealing and false charges, and think it very hard to be accused without cause. We should not be flesh and blood if we did not wish to have the good opinion of our neighbors. It is always unpleasant to be spoken against, and forsaken, and lied about, and to stand alone. But there is no help for it. The cup which our Master drank must be drunk by His disciples. They must be "despised and rejected of men" (Isaiah 53:3). Let us set down that item last in our account. To be a Christian it will cost a man the favor of the world.... Surely a Christian should be willing to give up anything which stands between him and heaven. A religion that costs nothing is worth nothing! A cheap Christianity, without a cross, will prove in the end a useless Christianity, without a crown.

Not a Fan – Teen Edition: Kyle Idleman video (9:41) at https://www.youtube.com/watch?v=duR4i6pg5y0 (accessed January 21, 2016) and *Not a Fan* – Teen Edition: Shelbi Draper video (19:25) at https://www.youtube.com/watch?v=OXcH8eEQrjc (accessed January 21, 2016).

Excerpt:

Followers ... understand that...

...There is no forgiveness without repentance.
...There is no salvation without surrender.
...There is no life without death.
...There is no believing without following.

Chapter Two

Puberty – "Talking With Your Preteen About Puberty and Sexuality," a one-page article at http://www.focusonthefamily.ca/parenting/school-age/talking-with-your-pre-teen-about-puberty-and-sexuality (accessed April 14, 2014). Read this first, as parents, then you may wish to read it with your kids.

Parenting in a Sexualized Culture: Christian Solutions for the 21st Century Parent, a 64-page book for free download at http://purehope.net/wp-content/uploads/2015/11/PureParenting_Booklet_FIN_2014-1-1.pdf (accessed January 6, 2016).

"Comprehensive" sexuality education – *The War on Children: The Comprehensive Sexuality Education Agenda*, video (35:19) at https://vimeo.com/152728936 (accessed May 4, 2016).

Analysis: Ontario Health & Physical Education Curriculum More Controversial than Anticipated, by Phil Lees at http://peaceontario.com/wp-content/uploads/2015/03/Ontario-Sex-Ed-Curriculum-Is-more-Controversial-Than-Anticipated-4.pdf.

Excerpt:

Comprehensive sexuality education [CSE] programs seek to change society by changing sexual and gender norms and teaching youth to advocate for their sexual rights. Most CSE programs promote acceptance of diverse sexual identities and orientations and enlist youth in combating "homophobia" and "heterosexism." These CSE programs have an almost obsessive focus on sexual pleasure, instructing children and youth at the earliest ages on how to obtain sexual pleasure in a variety of ways. Some programs even encourage sexual exploration for children as young as age five.

Planned Parenthood, one of the largest purveyors of CSE programs in the United States explains on its website that sexuality education addresses "values exploration, safer sex, sexual attitudes and values, sexual orientation, and sexual pleasures".

This is what the Ontario curriculum is built upon. CSE providers claim that this approach leads to reduced teen pregnancies and reduced sexually transmitted infections. However there is not one implementation of a CSE program that has resulted in statistically significant reductions. As a matter of fact the contrary is the norm. In New Brunswick implemented CSE in 2004/05 and between 2006 and 2010 teen pregnancies increased 40 percent and teen STI rates increased 38 percent – when the teen pregnancy rates in the rest of the country [Canada] were decreasing.

New Jersey and Oregon have implemented CSE the longest (1980 and 1984). Between 2007 and 2011 teen STI rates increased 25.3 percent and 38 percent respectively (Centre for Disease Control), however states like Hawaii, that do not have any mandatory sex education had only a 5 percent increase in teen STI rates over the same period.

10 Things Parents Need to Know about the New Sex-ed, video (6:41) https://www.facebook.com/theimfc/?fref=photo (Accessed February 1, 2016).

Miriam Grossman, MD (2009) *You're Teaching My Child What? A Physician Exposes the Lies of Sex Education and How They Harm your Child* (Regnery).

Ontario Schools, Sex-Education curriculum exposed by Dr. Miriam Grossman, video (1:00:11) at https://www.youtube.com/watch?v=21YvYPD56-U (accessed September 10, 2015).

Miriam Grossman, MD (2012) lecture to NZ teachers and administrators re *You're Teaching My Child What?* video

(58:58) at http://www.youtube.com/watch?v=0IeKSCHXs-0 (accessed April 12, 2013).

11 Minutes – Ontario Sex Education Program SE1/EP3, video (12:12) at https://www.youtube.com/watch?v=sutA78u4F1I (accessed September 10, 2015).

9 Months in the Womb, video (4:36) https://www.youtube.com/watch?v=WH9ZJu4wRUE (accessed April 3, 2016).

Chapter Three

Menstruation – "Understanding Your Period and Menstrual Cycle," a two-page article at http://teens.webmd.com/girls-puberty-10/girls-menstrual-cycle (accessed April 14, 2014). You, as a mom, may wish to read alone, then with your daughter.

Conception – Your daughter's questions might be answered at http://www.webmd.com/baby/guide/understanding-conception; https://www.youtube.com/watch?v=vFfqLs94iHc video (2:46; accessed June 17, 2014).

Development in the womb – *National Geographic In The Womb Multiples*, video (1:28:42) https://www.youtube.com/watch?v=BoMQrVBxa_w (accessed June 17, 2014).

Love – "Matrimony: United in love, strengthened for service," a two-page article at http://www.usccb.org/about/justice-peace-and-human-development/upload/Marriage-handout.pdf (accessed June 15, 2014).

Chapter Four

Puberty for boys – "Preparing Your Son for Adolescence," a one-page article at http://www.focusonthefamily.ca/parenting/school-age/preparing-your-son-for-adolescence (accessed June 16, 2014). You, as a dad, may wish to read alone, then with your son.

Development in the womb – *National Geographic In The Womb Multiples,* video (1:28:42) at https://www.youtube.com/watch?v=BoMQrVBxa_w (accessed June 17, 2014).

Chapter Five

Ten Commandments – note that for Command #6 many kids' versions suggest, "Don't hurt anyone." The problem with that idea is that it gives some people the idea that they are entitled to never be disciplined in any way or criticized in anyway, lest their feelings be hurt. That notion can be abused to silence all dissent and critical thinking.

The Ten Commandments: Introduction, Dennis Praeger video (5:36), plus the next 10 videos at https://www.prageru.com/courses/religionphilosophy/ten-commandments-introduction (accessed July 4, 2015).

Chapter Six

Four loves– "Different Types of Love from the Bible" at http://www.whatchristianswanttoknow.com/different-types-of-love-from-the-bible-a-christian-study/#ixzz31XIlaBjg; "The Four Loves" http://en.wikipedia.org/wiki/The_Four_Loves (accessed June 17, 2014).

Eros in married love – *David Pawson: Song of Songs,* video at https://www.youtube.com/watch?v=Z1OL6YX6B78 video (accessed June 17, 2014).

Consider Song of Songs 1:2–4 (Solomon's bride); 1:2–11(Solomon); 1:12–14 (his bride); 1:15(Solomon); 1:16–17; 2:1 (his bride); 2:2 (Solomon); 2:3–14, 16–17 (his bride); 4:11–15 (Solomon); 4:16 (his bride); 5:1 (Solomon); 3:1–4 (his bride); 4:7 (Solomon); 5:2–8 (his bride).

Made for Each Other: Sexual Difference is Essential to Marriage, video (12:24) "...Protecting and promoting marriage as the union of one man and one woman isn't arbitrary or discriminatory. Rather, it's a matter of justice, truth, love, and real freedom. Only a man and a woman – at every level of their identity: biological, physiological, emotional, social, spiritual – are capable of authentically speaking the language of married love, that is, the language of total self-gift, open to the gift of the other and the gift of life...." http://www.marriageuniqueforareason.org/sexual-difference-video/ (accessed June 17, 2014).

"Does Sex Have Meaning? (And Who Can Really Say?)," article at http://familyinamerica.org/journals/winter-2014/does-sex-have-meaning-and-who-can-really-say/#.U9-4eGNeI8A (accessed June 18, 2014).

What is Marriage? Ryan T. Anderson, video (55:57) at https://www.youtube.com/watch?v=YWIhZ5xJJaQ (accessed June 18, 2014).

"Making Sense of Marriage" video (9:54) at https://www.youtube.com/watch?v=an2TU58LITE (accessed May 3, 2016).

Pure Intimacy – an abundance of resources on many aspects of moral/spiritual brokenness at http://www.pureintimacy.org/about-us/ (accessed

August 27, 2014).

Purity Code – a youth development article available for free download at https://homeword.com/articles/shaping-spiritual-change-in-your-teenager/?cat=families#.Vy5eUnp5KiQ (accessed May 7, 2016)

Pure Foundations series by Jim Burns available at http://www.lifeway.com/n/Product-Family/Pure-Foundations (accessed August 27, 2014).

Inspiring Abstinence in Teens, video (28:25): https://vimeo.com/18732349 (accessed August 27, 2014).

Protect Your Purity, video (29:05): https://vimeo.com/90043157 (accessed August 28, 2014).

iparent.tv "an online resource that features hundreds of videos and posts to keep parents in the loop on all the latest tech fads that your kids might or might not be into." http://iparent.tv/about/ (accessed July 4, 2015).

Chapter Seven

The Holy Spirit – "What Does the Holy Spirit Do?" article at http://www.christianitytoday.com/iyf/advice/faithdoubt/what-does-holy-spirit-do.html (accessed April 3, 2016).

What Does the Holy Spirit Do? Alpha course video (25:39) at https://www.youtube.com/watch?v=caA52gA3pgA (accessed April 3, 2016).

Chapter Eight

Charitable Judging – "Charitable Judgements: An Antidote to Judging Others," an article by Ken Sande at http://www.rw360.org/2013/03/07/charitable-judgements-an-antidote-to-judging-others/ (accessed June 3, 2014).

"A Visit from James," David Kitz video (26:03) at https://www.youtube.com/watch?t=626&v=IhmDNHHhiIs (accessed June 15, 2015).

Sex Before Marriage – "The Mystery of Marriage" http://pafamily.org/wp-content/uploads/2014/08/The_Mystery_of_Marriage_by_Dr_Al_Mohler.pdf (accessed August 6, 2014).

"Waiting till the wedding night – getting married the right way," a one-page article at http://www.foxnews.com/opinion/2012/09/14/staying-celibate-before-marriage-was-best-thing-ive-ever-done/ (accessed August 6, 2014).

"How Can I Keep My Boyfriend Pure?" a two-page article at http://www.premaritalsex.info/how-can-i-keep-my-boyfriend-pure/#at_pco=smlwn-1.0&at_si=53e17896a31b41f5&at_ab=per-2&at_pos=0&at_tot=1 (accessed August 5, 2014).

"God's Design for Sex," a wealth of print & video resources at http://www.pureintimacy.org/gods-design-for-sex/ (accessed December 28, 2014).

Wait Until Marriage To Have Sex, Mark Gungor video (8:47) at https://www.youtube.com/watch?v=jL1l9ZtGC2w.

The War on Children: Exposing the Comprehensive Sexuality Education Agenda, video (36:12) at https://vimeo.com/152728936 (accessed February 28, 2016).

Healthy, Happy and Hot: A Young Person's Guide to their Rights, Sexuality and living with HIV, a 20-page free secular ebooklet by Planned Parenthood, pushed by Comprehensive Sex Ed at http://www.ippf.org/sites/default/files/healthy_happy_hot.pdf (accessed July 26, 2014). Use with caution.

Kay Arthur – Pt 1 – Her Story of Sexual Sin & Freedom in Christ, video (28:29) at https://vimeo.com/36707288 (accessed August 6, 2014).

STIs – Click on each STI and read useful information at http://intheknowpeel.ca/stiaids/list.htm (accessed June 28, 2014). Useful information on HIV/AIDS at http://healthycanadians.gc.ca/health-sante/disease-maladie/hiv-vih-eng.php (accessed July 26, 2014).

"Slideshow: Pictures and Facts About STDs" at http://www.webmd.com/sexual-conditions/ss/slideshow-std-pictures-and-facts?ecd=wnl_spr_050216&ctr=wnl-spr-050216_nsl-promo-4_title&mb=B8m4hc09oJbLQ9NOCKK0YOHnVev1imbCFA7o%2fIcRB08%3d (accessed May 2, 2016).

Chapter Nine

Pornography – "Porn Kills Love," one of six excellent one-page research papers on porn at http://fightthenewdrug.org/porn-kills-love/ (accessed November 22, 2015).

The Porn Pandemic: The Devastating Effects on Children, Family and Society, video (27:59): https://www.youtube.com/watch?v=NJ1ExvcsyLk (accessed August 6, 2014).

Why Is Porn a Growing Problem, video with Dr. Jill Manning (1:57) at https://www.youtube.com/watch?v=7avqQjhUMuY (accessed December 25, 2015).

The Porn-Free Family Plan http://www.challies.com/articles/the-porn-free-family-plan (Accessed May 7, 2017)

Testimony of a Former Underage Porn User, video (28:31): http://vimeo.com/album/69358/video/20138913 (Accessed August 6, 2014)

Current articles on porn available free at: http://www.covenanteyes.com/blog/ and https://www.netnanny.com/learn_center/article/ (accessed August 19, 2014).

"McAfee Safe Eyes 6.1.123 Review" at http://parental-software-review.toptenreviews.com/mcafee-safe-eyes-review.html (accessed January 6, 2016).

"Online Safety Cards for Kids' Technology Gifts," free downloads at https://www.fosi.org/good-digital-parenting/online-safety-cards-kids-technology-gifts/ (accessed January 6, 2016).

Over 60 videos on male porn addictions conquered at http://purepassion.us/index.php/pure-passion-tv/pornography-sex-addiction-male (accessed November 13, 2014).

A selection of videos critiquing porn at https://www.xxxchurch.com/videocat/live-events (accessed February 18, 2014).

"Pornography Info Parent Guide" at https://www.xxxchurch.com/get-help/porn-addiction-help-for-parents/critical-issues/pornography (accessed February 18, 2014).

"Pornography: Poisoning Marital Intimacy," article at http://www.premaritalsex.info/pornography-poisoning-marital-intimacy/#at_pco=smlwn-1.0&at_si=53e17d73d241f712&at_ab=per-4&at_pos=0&at_tot=1 (accessed August 5, 2014).

Let's Talk: Man to Man, video with Dan Rossi (8:28) at

https://www.youtube.com/watch?v=HBXyFwiv5y8 (accessed November 5, 2014).

Over 700 videos in several languages with personal testimonies and investigative reports on subjects such as human trafficking, child prostitution, pornography addiction, homosexuality and child abuse are available at http://www.purepassion.us/ (accessed August 6, 2014).

"Top 10 Effects of Porn on Your Brain, Your Marriage, and Your Sex Life," article and videos at http://tolovehonorandvacuum.com/2014/03/effects-of-porn-on-your-marriage/ (accessed December 28, 2014).

"The Truth About Porn," article at http://unitedfamiliesinternational.wordpress.com/2014/08/11/the-truth-about-porn/ (accessed December 28, 2014).

The Harms Of Pornography, a free book guide to research at http://unitedfamilies.org/default.asp?contentID=34 (accessed December 28, 2014).

Over a dozen articles on conquering porn addiction, at http://www.pureintimacy.org/pornography-addiction/ (accessed December 28, 2014).

Your Brain on Porn, free Christian ebook at http://www.covenanteyes.com/brain-ebook/?utm_campaign=porn-stats (accessed December 29, 2014).

Pornified Culture: Haunted Selves and Hindered Society (Part 1), Julia Beasley video (1:02:12) at https://www.youtube.com/watch?v=wNHazVMQICY (accessed November 13, 2015).

Pornified Culture: Haunted Selves and Hindered Society (Part 2), Julia Beasley video (1:11:11) at https://www.youtube.com/watch?v=4aysTfvCaVw

(accessed November 13, 2015).

Likely no one knows how many porn sites are available on the Internet or how many people watch these or how much they watch these. But one website lists 64 "Best Porn Tube Sites," plus 16 "Top Adult Live Cam Sites," plus 26 "Top Pay Porn Sites", plus several other categories (http://sexpornlist.net/, accessed January 14, 2016). In one year, 2015, PornHub, likely the Internet's largest porn website, people watched *4,392,486,580 hours of porn* (*501,425 years*). People watched *87,849,731,608 porn videos.* (That amounts to 12 porn videos viewed for every single person on the planet.) https://www.lifesitenews.com/blogs/pornhub-just-released-their-2015-statistics.-and-its-sickening (accessed January 13, 2016). In this messed-up world we Christian parents need to empower our kids to grow up in Christ!

Judith Riesman (2010) *Sexual Sabotage: How One Mad Scientist Unleashed a Plague of Corruption and CONTAGION on America* (WND Books)

Kinsey Sex study Fraud (Part 2), video (9:57) at https://www.youtube.com/watch?v=dud_se0unkQ (accessed July 12, 2015).

The Children of Table 34 (Part 1), video (10:00) at https://www.youtube.com/watch?v=vltmeBPKAAo; Part 2 (10:00) at https://www.youtube.com/watch?v=e-CW9kh6spo; Part 3 (9:26) at https://www.youtube.com/watch?v=xsa1RiVCoB8 (accessed July 12, 2015).

Contraceptives – An innovative website www.teachingsexualhealth.ca developed by Alberta (secular) educators and health professionals. "Our goal is to enhance excellence in education by providing teachers with evidence-based sexual health education background and delivery methods, current lesson plans and activities, and comprehensive resources." A good seven-page summary of the main contraception options with a few pros and cons for each and several links to responsible demonstrations is at http://teachers.teachingsexualhealth.ca/wp-content/uploads/Birth-Control-Kit.pdf (accessed July 15, 2014). You may also like to see their 12-page "Talking to Children about Sexuality: Parent Package (7-12 years old)" at http://parents.teachingsexualhealth.ca/topics/downloads/TSH-Parent-Package-7-12-2016.pdf (accessed July 15, 2014).

"Effectiveness of Family Planning Methods," Centers for Disease Control and Prevention http://www.cdc.gov/reproductivehealth/UnintendedPregnancy/PDF/Contraceptive_methods_508.pdf.

"How Effective Are Birth Control Methods?" article at http://www.cdc.gov/reproductivehealth/unintendedpregnancy/contraception.htm (accessed August 7, 2014).

Abortion issues – *Abortion Procedures & Injuries,* a video (16:24) that uses computer-generated animation to depict in 3-D the two most common surgical abortion procedures used under 20 weeks gestation at https://www.youtube.com/watch?v=v_apjhI3SHY (accessed July 30, 2014).

Post-Abortion Suffering: A Psychiatrist Looks at the Effects of Abortion, a booklet at http://downloads.frc.org/EF/EF10B09.pdf (accessed July 31, 2014).

Planned Parenthood Uses Partial Birth Abortions to Sell Baby Parts, video (8:51) at https://www.youtube.com/watch?t=288&v=jjxwVuozMnU (accessed July 14, 2015).

"Quick and Easy Guide to the Planned Parenthood Videos" at http://thefederalist.com/2015/09/29/a-quick-and-easy-guide-to-the-planned-parenthood-videos/ (accessed October 5, 2015).

Planned Parenthood Practices, video (7:33) in which abortion survivor Gianna Jessen testifies before the House Judiciary Committee, at http://www.c-span.org/video/?c4550358/gianna-jessen (accessed September 13, 2015).

Silent No More Awareness Campaign, stories of abortion experiences at http://www.silentnomoreawareness.org/plannedparenthood/planned-parenthood-testimony-quotes-july-2015.pdf (accessed August 12, 2015).

"Under the Radar Violence in the Conflict Over Abortion" at http://www.prolifeamerica.com/Under-the-Radar-Violence-in-the-Conflict-Over-Abortion.pdf (accessed July 31, 2014).

Late Term Abortionist George Tiller's Shocking Abortion Orientation Tape, video (12:56) at https://www.youtube.com/watch?v=6vog0aqpEAs (accessed July 31, 2014). Tiller repeats, "The woman is the patient, the fetus is the problem" in an attempt to rationalize the killing and shifting the blame over to the woman.

Behind the Mask: Interview with former abortionist, Dr. Anthony Levatino, video (10:00) at https://www.youtube.com/watch?v=F2pqZaQWlec (accessed July 31, 2014).

Doctor Who Did 1,200 Abortions Tells Congress to Ban Them, video (6:06) at https://www.youtube.com/watch?v=53tzMV9OmvY (accessed July 31, 2014).

"Our Five Surprises After Abortion" http://www.abbyjohnson.org/abbyjohnson/our-five-surprises-after-abortion (Accessed August 5, 2014).

An Overview of Abortion, video (2:45) at https://www.youtube.com/watch?v=NudvtDdc1Vk&list=UUqmNXuT6zlHpz3mCdXVCohw (Accessed August 5, 2014).

The Case Against Abortion: Prenatal Development, video (3:10) at https://www.youtube.com/watch?v=x-6VLUVglG8 (accessed August 5, 2014).

The Appointment – A Mother's Choice, video (6:32) at https://www.youtube.com/watch?v=PfAsNR2WXe0#t=22 (accessed November 18, 2014).

The Abortion Question, Dennis Praeger video (5:20) at https://www.prageru.com/courses/political-science/most-important-question-about-abortion (accessed November 7, 2015).

Sexual abuse issues – *How Do We Keep Our Kids Safe From Sexual Abuse*? video (8:29) at https://www.youtube.com/watch?v=noNhk3wGPxg&index=9&list=PL0ewHXE9hC7Qh3rSNyH67zvkoK3Sp75se (accessed November 18, 2014).

Why are sex offenders able to get away with it? video (8:31) at https://www.youtube.com/watch?v=B9_-nN4bUCw&index=2&list=PL0ewHXE9hC7Qh3rSNyH67zvkoK3Sp75se (accessed November 18, 2014).

Same-sex issues – "Same-sex Science," Stanton Jones article at http://www.firstthings.com/article/2012/01/same-sex-science (accessed November 18, 2014).

How Bad is Homosexual Practice According to Scripture? Robert Gagnon at:

http://www.robgagnon.net/articles/HomosexHowBadIsIt.pdf (accessed November 18, 2014).

Robert Gagnon, (2001) *The Bible and Homosexual Practice: Texts and Hermeneutics* (Abingdon).

"God's Design for Human Sexual Behavior" Robert Gagnon video, part two (26:34): https://www.youtube.com/watch?v=bG3nEH5Jn-A (accessed May 2, 2016)

Jesus, Scripture, and the Myth of New Knowledge Arguments about Homosexual Unions, Robert Gagnon video (76:40) at https://www.youtube.com/watch?v=iQMfnA_APoo (accessed June 20, 2014).

Challenges and Hope 2015 Restored Hope Conference, Robert Gagnon video (42:59) at https://www.youtube.com/watch?v=pIoCs6e-NFg (Accessed January 20, 2016)

Understanding Same-sex Attraction, video (32:11) at https://www.youtube.com/watch?v=jJhyzqdzpnM (accessed June 20, 2014).

Homosexuality 101, Dr. Julie Harren Hamilton video (38:23) at https://www.youtube.com/watch?v=C54CIxm-w44 (accessed December 5, 2015); shorter, older version (17:09) at https://www.youtube.com/watch?v=Lvb6ELLudvU (accessed December 5, 2015).

Lessons from the Sexuality Ministry Front, Stanton Jones video (42:40) at http://www.dts.edu/thetable/play/stanton-jones-chapel-on-homosexuality-and-church/ (accessed November 18, 2014).

"The Genetics of Same-Sex Attraction," a two-page article by Stanton Jones at http://www.firstthings.com/blogs/firstthoughts/2012/01/the-genetics-of-same-sex-attraction (accessed

November 18, 2014).

Stan Jones Discusses Homosexuality in the Context of Christian Sexual Ethics, video Part One (19:20) at http://www.dts.edu/thetable/play/discussing-homosexuality-sexuality-together/, Part Two (22:01) at http://www.dts.edu/thetable/play/homosexuality-part-2/; "Part Three" (16:52) at http://www.dts.edu/thetable/play/homosexuality-part-3/ (accessed August 8, 2014).

"Supreme Court's Re-definition of Marriage," article by W.L. Craig at http://www.reasonablefaith.org/supreme-courts-re-definition-of-marriage (accessed July 6, 2015).

What Does Science Reveal about Homosexuality? Dr. Brad Harrub video (30:10) at https://www.youtube.com/watch?v=yMcowZwrIU4 (accessed August 8, 2014).

Josh McDowell - Liberty University Convocation, video (37:24) at https://www.youtube.com/watch?v=Sd8pJuACRwY (accessed August 8, 2014).

Gay Activist Finds Christ, Charlene Cothan video (23:13) at https://www.youtube.com/watch?v=uQGA-n4JyOY (accessed August 3, 2014).

"Why Homosexual Love Stories Don't Have Happy Endings," a one-page article at http://www.charismanews.com/opinion/heres-the-deal/43893-why-homosexual-love-stories-don-t-have-happy-endings (accessed June 20, 2014).

"Sexuality and Same-sex Relationships" audio (42:13) https://www.bethinking.org/sexuality-and-samesex-relationships (accessed April 28, 2016).

Chapter Ten

Gay issues – *Rosaria Butterfield: Repentance & Renewal*, video (47:38) at https://www.youtube.com/watch?v=BBX8_vhu4Xw (accessed February 7, 2016).

Secret Thoughts of an Unlikely Convert, Dr. Rosaria Champagne Butterfield video (41:16) at https://www.youtube.com/watch?v=EoFmwsOCd6o (accessed February 5, 2016).

Is It Okay To Be Gay? A Candid Conversation on Christians and Same-Sex Attraction, video (41:58) at: https://www.youtube.com/watch?v=NJdEZv_24Uk (accessed February 7, 2016).

"The 'Trojan Couch:' How the Mental Health Associations Misrepresent Science," a 24-page article by Jeffrey Satinover, MD, PhD at http://factsaboutyouth.com/wp-content/uploads/TheTrojanCouchSatinover.pdf (accessed August 14, 2014).

Gay science is all fake, how gays control psychology, video by APA ex-president, N. A. Cummings (9:19) at https://www.youtube.com/watch?v=7NyX5CxGraE (accessed August 8, 2014).

Making Gay Okay: How Rationalizing Homosexual Behavior Is Changing Everything, video (10:05) at https://www.youtube.com/watch?v=sXrfImNeip0 (accessed July 28, 2014).

The Kinsey Syndrome, video (2:44:11) at: https://www.youtube.com/watch?v=j9ztmp1yDq8 (accessed May 2, 2013).

"Are People Really 'Born Gay'?" http://www.pureintimacy.org/a/are-people-really-born-gay/ (accessed September 25, 2013).

Such Were Some of You, video (6:37) at https://vimeo.com/78285817 (accessed July 14, 2014).

"The Health Risks of Gay Sex," a 31-page article by John R.

Diggs, Jr., M.D. at http://www.catholiceducation.org/en/marriage-and-family/sexuality/the-health-risks-of-gay-sex.html (accessed December 31, 2009.)

Rod Arquette hosts Heritage Foundation's Ryan T. Anderson, the Nation's Foremost Marriage Advocate, video (32:22) at https://www.youtube.com/watch?v=hm01jciJ3og#t=338 (accessed April 2, 2014).

Acceptance of Homosexuality in Christianity-Ravi Zacharias Answers Question: settled! video (9:02) at: https://www.youtube.com/watch?v=nx7ALlEtg2c (accessed April 2, 2014).

Should Marriage Be Limited To One Man And One Woman? video (4:54) at https://www.youtube.com/watch?v=utph8ba8koo (accessed July 1, 2015).

Cultural Imperialism, video (32:22) at https://www.youtube.com/watch?v=YWwRnbv2BOo (accessed August 16, 2014).

"Americans Have No Idea How Few Gay People There Are," article, *The Atlantic* http://www.theatlantic.com/politics/archive/2012/05/americans-have-no-idea-how-few-gay-people-there-are/257753/ (accessed April 17, 2015).

What Does the Bible Really Teach about Homosexuality, video by Kevin DeYoung (1:02:54) at https://www.crossway.org/blog/2015/04/what-does-the-bible-really-teach-about-homosexuality/ (accessed April 17, 2015).

Sexuality and Gender: Findings from the Biological, Psychological and Social Sciences by Lawrence S, Myer and Paul McHugh, a 143-page report on over 200 peer-reviewed studies painstakingly documenting what scientific research shows *and does not show* about sexuality and gender http://www.thenewatlantis.com/docLib/20160819_TNA50SexualityandGender.pdf (Accessed August 22, 2016).

Transgender issues – *Miriam Grossman, MD Interview*, video (41:12) at https://www.youtube.com/watch?t=75&v=_b_2CxHdd-8 (accessed April 12, 2013)

"Transgender Americans Face High Suicide Risk," a three-page article at http://www.nbcnews.com/id/40279043/ns/health-health_care/#.U9bZuLFeI8A (Accessed July 28, 2014)

Talking about Bruce Jenner, video (4:17) at http://www.str.org/videos/talking-about-bruce-jenner#.VYBk3UZVXMd (accessed June 16, 2015).

The Transgender: Normalizing MENTAL ILLNESS, video (15:59) at https://www.youtube.com/watch?v=aDAU3SPYFsA&feature=youtu.be (accessed April 4, 2016).

"The Battle Over Bathrooms," article at http://www.mercatornet.com/conjugality/view/the-battle-over-bathrooms/17849 (accessed April 5, 2016).

Intersexuality – "What is 'intersexuality' and how should Christians respond?" article at http://www.pureintimacy.org/w/what-is-intersexuality-and-how-should-christians-respond/ (accessed April 5, 2016).

Drugs – "How Does Marijuana Affect You?" article at http://www.webmd.com/mental-health/addiction/marijuana-use-and-its-effects

(accessed August 23, 2014).
"About Marijuana" at http://healthycanadians.gc.ca/healthy-living-vie-saine/substance-abuse-toxicomanie/controlled-drugs-substances-controlees/marijuana/about-au-sujet-eng.php (accessed November 12, 2014).
Marijuana – Effects on the Brain, video (2:26) at http://www.check123.com/videos/7747-marijuana-effects-on-the-brainin (accessed November 22, 2015).

Chapter Twelve

Truth – *Four Lies the Culture Tells About the Truth*, J. Warner Wallace video (28:00) at https://www.youtube.com/watch?v=8HXRFG7nklI (accessed December 20, 2015).
The Case For Truth, J. Warner Wallace video (52:29) at https://www.youtube.com/watch?v=dSHVAKrH7CM (accessed December 20, 2015).
Why Are You A Christian? J. Warner Wallace video (28:00) https://www.youtube.com/watch?v=P1Aew6QT1qg (accessed December 20, 2015).
The Truth About Sex According to God (Part 2), Kay Arthur video (20:06) at https://www.youtube.com/watch?v=7Yeg8aGCEbw (Accessed June 3, 2014)

Grace – *Such Were Some of You*, trailer video (2:44) at http://suchweresomeofyou.org/ (accessed June 3, 2014)
How to Rise Above Abuse, June Hunt video (22:27) at https://www.youtube.com/watch?v=CP_fkmom_TI (accessed June 3, 2014).

DTM 2014 London: Dr Christopher Rosik, video (26:37) at https://www.youtube.com/watch?v=-ijV8YEr6fg (accessed August 8, 2014)

Journal of Human Sexuality, Vol. 1, NARTH (128 pages) pdf at http://scholar.google.ca/scholar?q=Journal+of+Human+Sexuality&hl=en&as_sdt=0&as_vis=1&oi=scholart&sa=X&ei=4C_oU4-tDZGlyQSW9YCQCg&ved=0CBwQgQMwAA (accessed December 9, 2013).

"Prohibiting Sex Purchasing and Ending Trafficking: The Swedish Prostitution Law," a 25-page research paper at http://www.prostitutionresearch.com/pdfs/Waltman_ProhibitingSexPurchasingEndingTrafficking_MichJofInt percent27lLaw33 percent282011 percent29.pdf

Chapter Thirteen

Choosing friends – "Choose your Friends Carefully," article at http://www.bible-knowledge.com/choose-your-friends-carefully/ (accessed March 30, 2016).

Chapter Fourteen

Choosing a church – "How To Choose A Church: 7 Things To Look For," article at http://www.whatchristianswanttoknow.com/how-to-choose-a-church-7-things-to-look-for/ (accessed April 5, 2016)

PARENTS' SUPPLEMENT

1. If you have any comments, questions, or feedback, please tell us at www.growingupinchrist.com "Contacts" page.

2. If you like this book, please tell your friends and write an honest review at your nearest Amazon site (e.g., www.Amazon.com or www.Amazon.ca, etc.) and anywhere else you think this book might be of interest.

3. Also please "like" us on Facebook at

   "Growing Up In Christ"(Education)

4. Watch for other titles in this series at www.growingupinchrist.com

Book 1: *A is for Adam,* full colored sketches and nursery rhymes on alphabet letters.	*A is for Adam Coloring Book,* same rhymes and text as Book 1	Book 2: *The Kids of Messed Up Woods,* a "first novel" for ages 5-8; with black and white art	Book 3: This book you are now reading	Book 4: *Dealing with Doubts and Differences,* essays for teens (ages 13-19) on their truth issues	Book 5: *Deciding Right from Wrong,* essays for teens (ages 13-19) on ethical issues

ABOUT THE AUTHOR

Al Hiebert has a passion to equip Christian parents to empower their kids to grow up in Christ in our messed-up world. With friends, including Costarican artist Claudia Castro Castro, they have formed Growing Up In Christ, Inc.

Al is married to Lorna, his high school sweetheart. They have two married children, and three grandchildren, all loving Jesus.

Al graduated MA at TEDS and PhD at NYU. He taught high school math and science, then philosophy and theology at Providence University College and Seminary (MB) 1969-95, then philosophy, theology, and leadership at Briercrest Seminary (1996-2003). "Uncle Al" served as director of Red Rock Bible Camp 1964-71, as college dean 1974-94, as seminary dean 1996-99, as director of the Briercrest branch campus MA at OM India 1996-2003, and as the first executive director of Christian Higher Education Canada 2007-10. Besides many articles in magazines and newspapers and several journal articles, Al has published (2005) *Character with Competence Education* and *Hiebert Heritage to 2010*.

In 1973 Al and Lorna moved a 1924 railroad station to a wooded site near Kleefeld, MB and renovated it for their home. They now live in Steinbach. MB. Al regularly comments on ethics and lifestyle issues in many media.

---

[1] Jerrold S. Greenberg, Clint E. Bruess, and Sara B. Oswalt (2014) *Exploring the dimensions of human sexuality* (5th ed.) 79.

[2] http://purehope.net/wp-content/uploads/2015/11/PureParenting_Booklet_FIN_2014-1-1.pdf (accessed January 6, 2016).

[3] https://www.netnanny.com/blog/internet-safety-the-biggest-mistake-smart-parents-make/ (accessed November 22, 2015).

[4] Romans 3:23.

[5] 1 John 1:9; 1Corinthians 10:13.

[6] 2 Corinthians 10:3–5.

[7] Genesis 1–3.

[8] Romans 8:18–24.

[9] https://www.youtube.com/watch?v=8HXRFG7nklI (accessed December 20, 2015).

[10] 1 Peter 1:13–25.

[11] http://www.blueletterbible.org/faq/don_stewart/don_stewart_1284.cfm (accessed March 27, 2014).

[12] Mark 10:18.

[13] Exodus 3:5.

[14] Exodus 26:33.

[15] Exodus 20:8–11.

[16] Exodus 29:44.

[17] Isaiah 6:3–5.

---

[18] Ryle, John Charles, *Holiness: Its Nature, Hindrances, Difficulties, and Roots* (London: James Clarke & Co.) and http://www.monergism.com/4-costs-becoming-christian (accessed April 14, 2014).

[19] http://quoteinvestigator.com/2013/02/24/truth-revolutionary/ (accessed May 10, 2015).

[20] http://thewellpgh.org/ (accessed May 10, 2015).

[21] There are over 50,000 videos on YouTube on this question. One of the best is by Mark Bromley (caution: university-level language) at: https://www.youtube.com/watch?v=oavnI5h5lxg (53:27; accessed January 21, 2016).

[22] https://www.youtube.com/watch?v=ii4QmFA--gs (20:18; accessed May 10, 2015) Scientific proof of God – Dr. William Lane Craig (debate excerpt).

[23] http://kidshealth.org/kid/word/a/word_acne.html#cat20190 (accessed April 12, 2014).

[24] Genesis 1:26–28.

[25] http://www.lifehack.org/articles/communication/the-way-people-treat-you-statement-about-who-they-are-human-being.html (accessed March 31, 2014).

[26] http://www.belove.world/ (accessed January 10, 2016).

[27] http://assessment.everydayhealth.com/how-much-you-know-about-your-bodys-amazing-hormones/# (accessed May 4, 2016).

[28] http://assessment.everydayhealth.com/how-much-you-know-about-your-bodys-amazing-hormones/# (accessed May 4, 2016).

[29] Adam and Eve fell from their original state of moral and spiritual innocence by disobeying God's command not to eat of the tree of the knowledge of good and evil. That sinful pattern has been practiced by all humans ever since. Hence, we are all guilty of sin ("messed up") and subject to death, the end of our life on earth and eternal separation from God. But God in His infinite love, mercy, and grace sent Christ, His Son, to earth to take on Himself all human sin and justly pay its penalty in His atoning death on Calvary's cross. He did this to "redeem" (rescue, save) from sin's penalty and power all who repent of their sin and by faith accept His gift of total forgiveness and new abundant life. This "good news" (gospel) message is the core theme of the Bible as the only means to clean up our mess of sinful rebellion. It has many practical implications, including our following Christ in every dimension of our lives and lovingly care for the poor, the needy of all sorts, and our messed-up natural environment. Many in our culture mess up many of these biblical truths with distortions and lies of all sorts. Everyone needs to be warned of these as they grow up and hopefully embrace as their own the truths taught in the Bible. (Compare, "If we never meet again" at http://litmin.org/store/products.php?prodid=1014&do=list and "The Gospel Message," an 11-minute video at http://www.godtube.com/watch/?v=77K7Y7NX).

Related Scriptures include (but are not limited to): Isaiah 64:4–5; John 1:1–3, 14, 18; 3:16–18, 36; 5:24; 10:10; 14:1–3, 6; 20:26–31; Acts 4:10, 12; 16: 31;

Romans 1:21; 3:23–24; 5: 8, 12, 17; 6:23; 10:13; 1 Corinthians 15:1–8; 2 Corinthians. 5:21; Ephesians 2:8-9; Hebrews 10:11–12, 23; 1 John 5:11.

[30] See "Not a Fan" video (19:25) at https://www.youtube.com/watch?v=OXcH8eEQrjc (accessed January 21, 2016).

[31] Genesis 1:26, 27.

[32] http://www.biblestudytools.com/lexicons/greek/kjv/teleios.html (accessed April 24, 2014).

[33] Matthew 16:24–25.

[34] https://www.goodreads.com/quotes/4342-all-the-darkness-in-the-world-cannot-extinguish-the-light (accessed May 4, 2016).

[35] Romans 1: 18–21; 2: 14–15.

[36] Genesis 1:27; 2:24; 5:2. Notice how Jesus appeals without question to the authority of Scripture, including the Adam and Eve story of early Genesis.

[37] Revelation 19:6–9.

[38] Genesis 1:26–27.

[39] Ken Sande, "Charitable Judgments: An Antidote to Judging Others," http://www.rw360.org/2013/03/07/charitable-judgements-an-antidote-to-judging-others/ (accessed June 3, 2014).

[40] Sande, "Charitable Judgment."

[41] http://www.charismanews.com/opinion/in-the-line-of-fire/44805-universalism-is-next-for-the-soft-love-crowd (accessed July 30, 2014).

[42] https://www.goodreads.com/quotes/673583-the-further-a-society-drifts-from-truth-the-more-it (accessed July 7, 2014).

[43] http://www.premaritalsex.info/sex-in-the-real-world/ (accessed August 5, 2014).

[44] http://themattwalshblog.com/2014/08/05/i-will-not-teach-my-kids-about-safe-sex/#hX32clX1TFe8GBBD.99 (accessed August 6, 2014).

[45] http://www.theglobeandmail.com/life/the-hot-button/couples-who-wait-report-better-sex-lives/article1847555/ (accessed August 7, 2014).

[46]http://www.cdc.gov/reproductivehealth/UnintendedPregnancy/PDF/Contraceptive_methods_508.pdf and http://www.cdc.gov/reproductivehealth/unintendedpregnancy/contraception.htm (accessed August 7, 2014).

[47]http://www.un.org/en/development/desa/population/publications/pdf/popfacts/popfacts_2013-9.pdf (accessed July 7, 2014).

[48] http://www.nhs.uk/conditions/contraception-guide/pages/contraception.aspx (accessed July 14, 2014).

[49] Miriam Grossman (2009) *You're Teaching My Child What?: A Physician Exposes the Lies of Sex Ed and How They Harm Your Child* (Regnery), 111. This book is all based on medical science. The writer is Jewish (not a Christian).

[50] http://www.miriamgrossmanmd.com/wp-content/uploads/2012/11/sex_ed_report.pdf (accessed July 14, 2014).

[51] https://www.youtube.com/watch?v=49I2df_4PaI (accessed August 13, 2014).

[52] http://thehill.com/blogs/congress-blog/healthcare/214865-planned-parenthood-gives-sm-advice#ixzz3AIEXBtju (accessed August 13, 2014).

[53] At http://www.webmd.com/search/search_results/default.aspx?query=sti (accessed June 29, 2014) are 136 articles on STIs.

[54] http://www.who.int/mediacentre/factsheets/fs110/en/ (accessed June 28, 2014).

[55] http://www.who.int/gho/hiv/en/ (accessed July 5, 2014).

[56] http://www.webmd.com/women/health-myths-know-truth?page=5 (accessed June 29, 2014).

[57] http://www.who.int/mediacentre/factsheets/fs110/en/ (accessed May 5, 2016).

[58] http://kidshealth.org/teen/sexual_health/stds/std_myths.html#cat20017 (accessed June 29, 2014).

[59] http://www.miriamgrossmanmd.com/wp-content/uploads/2012/11/sex_ed_report.pdf (accessed July 14, 2014).

[60] https://www.youtube.com/watch?v=sXrfImNeip0 (accessed July 28, 2014).

[61] Sexual attraction to children is called pedophilia; sexual activity with family members is called incest.

[62] See "How do we keep our kids safe from sexual abuse?" video (8:29) https://www.youtube.com/watch?v=noNhk3wGPxg&index=9&list=PL0ewHXE9hC7Qh3rSNyH67zvkoK3Sp75se.

[63] http://www.familywatchinternational.org/fwi/policy_brief_porn.pdf (accessed August 17, 2014).

[64] https://vimeo.com/18732349 (accessed August 27, 2014).

[65] http://en.wikipedia.org/wiki/Neuroplasticity (accessed July 16, 2014).

[66] http://fightthenewdrug.org/porn-is-a-lie/ (accessed November 22, 2015).

[67] http://www.xxxchurch.com/parents/pornography.html (accessed July 5, 2014).

[68] http://fightthenewdrug.org/porn-kills-love/ (accessed November 22, 2015).

[69] https://www.youtube.com/watch?v=6NR86jX1SRI (accessed May 6, 2016).

[70] Kristen Jenson and Gail Poyner (2014) *Good Pictures Bad Pictures: Porn-Proofing Today's Young Kids*. Glen Cove Press. Kindle Edition.

[71] http://www.miriamgrossmanmd.com/wp-content/uploads/2012/11/sex_ed_report.pdf (accessed July 14, 2014).

[72] http://vimeo.com/album/69358 and https://vimeo.com/78285817 (accessed July 14, 2014). Note the 6:34 "Sizzle Reel" trailer that introduces a two-hour documentary "Such Were Some of You," which tells the story of 29 ex-gays, some who left that lifestyle with counselling, some without.

[73] http://www.webmd.com/sex/anal-sex-health-concerns (accessed July 16, 2014).

[74] http://www.webmd.com/sex/anal-sex-health-concerns (accessed July 16, 2014). Sodomy laws have made anal sex illegal in most of the world throughout history and still do in many parts today, see: https://en.wikipedia.org/wiki/Sodomy_law (accessed May 19, 2019).

[75] Grossman, *Teaching*, 83–97.

[76] Grossman, *Teaching*, 91.

[77] http://egale.ca/all/press-release-ysps-recommendations/ (accessed May 13, 2015).

[78] http://www.webmd.com/sex-relationships/features/4-things-you-didnt-know-about-oral-sex?page=2 (accessed July 16, 2014).

[79] Grossman, *Teaching*, 93.
[80] Grossman, *Teaching*, 116.
[81] Grossman, *Teaching*, 116.
[82] http://www.miriamgrossmanmd.com/wp-content/uploads/2012/11/sex_ed_report.pdf (accessed July 14, 2014).
[83] The terms "homosexual" and "heterosexual" were invented by Hungarian journalist Karl-Maria Kertbeny in 1869. He also first argued that these sexual preferences are inborn and unchangeable. http://en.wikipedia.org/wiki/Karl-Maria_Kertbeny (accessed August 17, 2014).
[84] http://www.narth.com/#!gay---born-that-way/cm6x (accessed March 8, 2015).
[85] http://www.narth.com/#!gay---born-that-way/cm6x (accessed March 8, 2015).
[86] http://www.firstthings.com/blogs/firstthoughts/2012/01/the-genetics-of-same-sex-attraction (accessed January 17, 2016).
[87] http://www.christopheryuan.com/main/flash/question5.swf (accessed December 23, 2015); http://www.mygenes.co.nz/PDFs/Ch10.pdf (accessed December 21, 2015): "In a nutshell, if you take pairs of identical twins in which one twin is homosexual, the identical co-twin (a monozygotic (MZ) twin) is usually *not* homosexual. That means, given that identical twins are always genetically identical, homosexuality cannot be genetically dictated. No-one is born gay. The predominant things that create homosexuality in one identical twin and not in the other have to be post-birth factors."
[88] http://www.cdc.gov/nchs/data/nhsr/nhsr077.pdf (accessed July 19, 2014).
[89] http://www.theatlantic.com/politics/archive/2012/05/americans-have-no-idea-how-few-gay-people-there-are/257753/ (accessed July 19, 2014).
[90] http://downloads.frc.org/EF/EF08L42.pdf (accessed August 12, 2014) and http://onenewsnow.com/culture/2012/11/12/pro-lesbian-study-uses-biased-statistics#.U_I_62NeJWy (accessed August 13, 2014).
[91] http://mirrorofjustice.blogs.com/files/shorts-taking-on-god.pdf (accessed April 20, 2013); http://www.lifesitenews.com/news/canadian-law-prof.-wants-provinces-to-force-queering-of-catholic-schools/ (accessed April 20, 2013); http://www.queerty.com/can-we-please-just-start-admitting-that-we-do-actually-want-to-indoctrinate-kids-20110512/#ixzz20KlAegpH (accessed February 22, 2015).
[92] http://egale.ca/every-class/ (accessed July 2, 2013). In 2016 the same research team released *The Every Teacher Project on LGBTQ-inclusive Education in Canada's K-12 Schools*. Out of some 633,000 Canadian K-12 teachers they similarly recruited 3,319 volunteers for their survey, most of whom favoured LGBTQ education. Of these some 473 (16%) respondents self-identified as LGBTQ and 81(3%) respondents self-identified as transgender. http://egale.ca/wp-content/uploads/2016/01/Every-Teacher-Project-Final-Report-WEB.pdf (accessed July 1, 2016)
[93]http://www.mercatornet.com/articles/view/is_the_gay_bullying_plague_in_our_schools_a_myth#sthash.rQz86s0P.dpuf (accessed August 26, 2014).

[94] http://dictionary.reference.com/browse/transgender?s=t (Accessed August 3, 2014)

[95] http://www.webmd.com/mental-health/gender-dysphoria (Accessed May 17, 2016)

[96] http://genderfluidsupport.tumblr.com/gender/ (Accessed Mark 8, 2016)

[97] http://dictionary.reference.com/browse/androgynous?s=t (Accessed August 15, 2014)

[98] http://www.urbandictionary.com/define.php?term=autosexual (Accessed August 15, 2014)

[99] http://www.livescience.com/9648-sex-change-operations-science-sociology-psychology.html (Accessed July 28, 2014)

[100] http://www.smithsonianmag.com/smart-news/there-are-372-trillion-cells-in-your-body-4941473/?no-ist and http://en.wikipedia.org/wiki/XY_sex-determination_system (Accessed May 12, 2015)

[101] http://www.breitbart.com/london/2015/12/28/transgender-fad-rapidly-spreading-primary-schools-clusters-emerging-children-copy-friends/ (Accessed December 29, 2015)

[102] https://thebridgehead.ca/2015/12/30/state-of-the-culture-the-year-we-abolished-reality/ (Accessed January 12, 2016)

[103] https://www.youtube.com/watch?v=JezK_w5MjTM and https://www.youtube.com/watch?v=BZBErJE37v8 (Accessed July 28, 2014)

[104] https://www.youtube.com/watch?v=63Sz_OHeOqk (Accessed July 28, 2014)

[105] http://online.wsj.com/articles/paul-mchugh-transgender-surgery-isnt-the-solution-1402615120 (Accessed August 22, 2014)

[106] http://www.thepublicdiscourse.com/2015/06/15145/ (Accessed April 29, 2016).

[107] http://www.cnsnews.com/news/article/michael-w-chapman/johns-hopkins-psychiatrist-transgender-mental-disorder-sex-change (Accessed December 31, 2015). See also the 143-page report on over 200 peer-reviewed studies in the biological, psychological, and social sciences, painstakingly documenting what scientific research shows *and does not show* about sexuality and gender at http://www.thenewatlantis.com/docLib/20160819_TNA50SexualityandGender.pdf (Accessed August 22, 2016).

[108] http://www.acpeds.org/the-college-speaks/position-statements/gender-ideology-harms-children?utm_source=email+marketing+Mailigen&utm_campaign=News+3.23.16&utm_medium=email (Accessed March 24, 2016).

[109] http://www.wnd.com/2014/07/a-gay-christian-advocate-sinks-his-own-ship/#Z44YD1KerYlDO8gW.99 (accessed July 24, 2014).

[110] https://www.youtube.com/watch?feature=player_embedded&v=YpQHGPGejKs#! (accessed August 14, 2014).

[111] http://apologiabyhendrikvanderbreggen.blogspot.ca/search/label/Homosexuality (accessed August 14, 2014).

---

112 https://www.youtube.com/watch?v=nx7ALlEtg2c (accessed May, 15, 2016).

113 https://www.youtube.com/watch?v=pIoCs6e-NFg (accessed January 20, 2016).

114https://www.youtube.com/watch?v=iQMfnA_APoo&list=UU2JPmy9Oi_5kAmaVPAInWFw (accessed May 15, 2015).

115 https://www.youtube.com/watch?v=BBX8_vhu4Xw at 43:12 (accessed January 19, 2016).

116 http://dictionary.reference.com/browse/bigot (accessed July 26, 2014).

117 http://dictionary.reference.com/browse/homophobe?s=t (accessed July 26, 2014).

118 http://narth.com/docs/coll-breiner.html (accessed April 28, 2013) .

119 Joe Dallas was a pastor of a gay church as a practising gay. He has since left the LGBTQ community and has written several books critical of that community's beliefs. He writes, "There's an intolerant, heavy-handed element of the modern gay-rights movement that seeks not only to normalize homosexuality, but to also silence anyone who resists their efforts." (Joe Dallas and Nancy Heche, eds. *The Compete Christian Guide to Understanding Homosexuality: A Biblical and Compassionate Response to Same-sex Attraction*, Harvest House, p.44).

120 http://factsaboutyouth.com/wp-content/uploads/What-research-shows-homosexuality.NARTH_.pdf (accessed August 14, 2014).

121 "Progressive psychiatrists, gay psychiatrists, and outside activists planned a disruption and sought the services of leftwing activist Frank Kameny, who turned for help to the New Left and non-accommodationist Gay Liberation Front. Kameny's cadre, with forged credentials provided by allies on the inside (some at the very top) broke into a special lifetime service award meeting. They grabbed the microphone, and Kameny declared 'Psychiatry is the enemy incarnate. Psychiatry has waged a relentless war of extermination against us.... We're rejecting you all as our owners. You may take this as our declaration of war.' Regardless, a few hours later, the promised panel discussion – presented by the same group of protesters – proceeded without objection by the APA." http://www.narth.org/docs/TheTrojanCouchSatinover.pdf (accessed August 14, 2014).

122 http://dailycaller.com/2014/03/19/nobody-is-born-that-way-gay-historians-say/#ixzz2yQNdDi9i (accessed April 9, 2014).

123 https://thereformedmind.wordpress.com/2012/06/14/is-gay-parenting-bad-for-the-kids/ (accessed April 12, 2013).

124 http://factsaboutyouth.com/wp-content/uploads/Superintendent-LetterC_3.311.pdf (accessed August 16, 2014).

125 http://www.charismanews.com/opinion/44691-former-homosexual-reveals-unmitigated-disaster-of-gay-marriage?utm_medium=MostPopularArticles_RightColBottom (Accessed July 26, 2014).

126http://scholar.google.ca/scholar?q=Journal+of+Human+Sexuality&hl=en&as_sdt=0&as_vis=1&oi=scholart&sa=X&ei=4C_oU4-

tDZGlyQSW9YCQCg&ved=0CBwQgQMwAA (accessed December 9, 2013)

[127] http://vimeo.com/purepassion/videos/sort:duration/format:thumbnail (accessed August 10, 2014). Their two-hour documentary *Such Were Some of You* chronicles the stories of 29 former homosexual men and women who say that Jesus Christ has transformed their lives. Experts in psychology (Dr. Julie Hamilton), biblical scholarship (Dr. Robert Gagnon), and ministry (Dr. Neil Anderson) add their voice to the claim that people have been leaving homosexuality for millennia. See trailer at http://suchweresomeofyou.org/ and review at http://www.pfox.org/new-documentary-with-numerous-ex-gays/ (accessed July 28, 2014).

[128] http://www.narth.com/#!gay---born-that-way/cm6x (accessed March 8, 2015).

[129] As of June, 2014 Pew Foundation listed 18 countries where same-sex marriage was legal in all or part of the country, see http://www.pewforum.org/2013/12/19/gay-marriage-around-the-world-2013/ (accessed August 20, 2014).

[130] http://www.marriageuniqueforareason.org/sexual-difference-video/ (Accessed June 17, 2014).

[131] https://www.youtube.com/watch?v=hm01jciJ3og#t=338 (accessed April 2, 2014).

[132] https://www.youtube.com/watch?v=hm01jciJ3og#t=338 (accessed April 2, 2014).

[133] https://www.youtube.com/watch?v=hm01jciJ3og#t=338 (accessed April 2, 2014).

[134] http://www.telegraph.co.uk/news/religion/11709442/Children-who-say-homosexuality-is-wrong-could-be-viewed-as-extremist-threat-Education-Secretary.html (accessed July 1, 2015).

[135] https://avemariaradio.net/i-cant-celebrate-but-it-doesnt-mean-i-hate-you/ (accessed July 18, 2015).

[136] http://radio.focusonthefamily.ca/broadcasts/accepting-my-true-identity-in-christ-part-2-of-2 (accessed January 29, 2016).

[137] The Bible is God's truth: "... the purpose of the church is to be the pillar and support of the truth..." – Charles Swindoll http://www.insight.org/broadcast/?ga=topnav-broadcast-L2 (accessed June 1, 2015).

[138] https://www.youtube.com/watch?v=26xNd78Duwo (17:14) (accessed November 7, 2014).

[139] 1 Corinthians 15:36

[140] http://gcmwatch.com/exhomosexual-videos/ video anthology of 225+ living witnesses – representing many nations – who have left homosexuality, bisexuality and lesbianism to follow Jesus Christ. (accessed November 7, 2014). In https://www.youtube.com/watch?v=BBX8_vhu4Xw (47:38; accessed January 17, 2016) Dr. Rosaria Butterfield tells of her journey from her roles as tenured university professor of English and women's

studies and faculty advisor to many campus LGBT clubs as a lesbian atheist to an evangelical Presbyterian pastor's wife and home-schooling mom, from teaching queer theory to studying biblical hermeneutics.

[141] http://www.christianpost.com/news/lifeways-true-love-waits-movement-to-launch-new-updated-sexual-purity-campaign-110046/cpf (accessed May 13, 2015).

[142] http://www.redletterbelievers.com/just-dont-agree-doesnt-mean-hate/ (accessed July 18, 2015).

[143] Kyle Idleman (2011) *Not a Fan: Becoming a Completely Committed Follower of Jesus*: (Zondervan).

[144] http://www.focusonthefamily.com/faith/faith-in-life/prayer/learning-from-the-prayer-life-of-jesus (accessed May 7, 2016).

[145] https://www.youtube.com/watch?v=9RftwrybUHI (accessed May 7, 2016); also Joe Solomon video (6:33) at https://www.youtube.com/watch?v=NeZvochYLu0 (accessed March 12, 2016).

[146]http://www.garyhabermas.com/articles/areopagus_jesusinspirationscripture/areopagus_jesusinspirationscripture.htm (accessed March 12, 2016).

[147] https://www.youtube.com/watch?v=WBYncNR0q9Q (accessed May 7, 2016)

[148] Most of these are adapted from http://www.webmd.com/ (accessed March 29, 2014) and from http://kidshealth.org/kid/word/ (accessed March 29, 2014).

[149] Kristen Jenson and Gail Poyner (2014) *Good Pictures Bad Pictures: Porn-Proofing Today's Young Kids*. Glen Cove Press. Kindle Edition.

[150] http://egale.ca/all/every-class/ (accessed July 3, 2013).